every day.

Fr. Dunn

PRAYERS FOR TODAY

To

the Mother of God
and Mother of us all

*"My soul gives praise to the Lord,
and my spirit rejoices in God my Savior."*

(Lk 1:46)

"Let the entire body of the faithful pour forth persevering prayer to the Mother of God and Mother of us all. Let them implore that she who aided the beginnings of the Church by her prayers may now, exalted as she is in heaven above all the saints and angels, intercede with her Son in the fellowship of all the saints. May she do so until all the peoples of the human family, whether they are honored with the name of Christian or whether they still do not know their Savior, are happily gathered together in peace and harmony into the one People of God, for the glory of the Most High and Undivided Trinity."

— *The Constitution on the Church, Second Vatican Council*

PRAYERS FOR TODAY

FIAT VOLUNTAS TUA

Originally compiled by Terence Cardinal Cooke
(1921-1983)

Revised and updated by
The Cardinal Cooke Guild

ALBA•HOUSE   NEW•YORK

SOCIETY OF ST. PAUL, 2187 VICTORY BLVD., STATEN ISLAND, NY 10314

Scripture quotations from the *New Revised Standard Version of the Bible* copyright @ 1989 by the Division of Christian Education of the National Council of the Churches of Christ in the United States of America and from *The Alba House Gospels: So You May Believe* copyright @ 1991 by the Society of St. Paul, Inc. and used with permission.

Nihil Obstat:
James T. O'Connor
Censor Librorum

Imprimatur:
✠ Patrick Sheridan, DD
Vicar General, Archdiocese of New York
July 4, 1991

The Nihil Obstat and Imprimatur are official declarations that a book or pamphlet is free of doctrinal or moral error. No implication is contained therein that those who have granted the Nihil Obstat and Imprimatur agree with the contents, opinions or statements expressed.

Produced and designed in the United States of America by the Fathers and Brothers of the Society of St. Paul, 2187 Victory Boulevard, Staten Island, New York 10314, as part of their communications apostolate.

ISBN: 0-8189-0628-6

Printing Information:

Current Printing - first digit	1	2	3	4	5	6	7	8	9	10

Year of Current Printing - first year shown

1991	1992	1993	1994	1995	1996	1997

PREFACE TO THE FIRST EDITION

The human events of our day can be faced peacefully only by men and women of prayer. Without prayer, our faith is weakened, our love grows cold, our hope becomes uncertain. It is my conviction that prayer should penetrate and pervade the believer's day. Prayer and life are, or ought to be, conterminous.

Yet prayer, like life itself, is a mystery. How readily we can identify with the disciples' plea to Jesus, "Lord, teach us how to pray." They wished to be able to pray as he prayed in the Holy Spirit and they knew that they needed help.

He taught them to say "our" Father. And he taught them also, by his day-to-day manner of life, the climate of his prayer, and his own need to pray. He prayed simply, directly, without affectation, with deep awareness of his Father's love and daily concern for him; and he prayed out of his own need to glorify his Father's name and to seek his Father's help so that he could do his Father's will.

The past years have brought a great renewal of positive interest in liturgical prayer. At the same time, all agree with the words of the Constitution on the Sacred Liturgy of the Second Vatican Council: "The spiritual life, however, is not limited solely to participation in the liturgy. The Christian is indeed called to pray with his brethren, but he must also enter into his chamber to pray to the Father in secret; yet more, according to the teaching of the Apostle, he should pray without ceasing" (n. 12).

While many questions remain about the scope, the manner, and even the proper concept of private or nonliturgical prayer, we must continue to move toward living and life-enriching answers, or else place our own spiritual growth in peril.

In presenting these private prayers and devotions, traditional as well as new prayers have been included to cover a wide range of needs and circumstances. I have tried to keep in mind that prayer should be a free expression of our gift of self to God, that all prayer is nourished by Sacred Scripture, and that, at least at times, a form of words helps to stimulate personal prayer.

I look upon *Prayers for Today* as a beginning. It is my own prayerful hope that it will assist the perhaps considerable number of people who at the moment are confused about prayer and are in need of encouragement. I also hope it will provoke thoughts and reflections which, in turn, will deepen our understanding of prayer and our union with God in the days to come.

— Terence Cardinal Cooke

INTRODUCTION TO THE SECOND EDITION

Cardinal Cooke often said that the best gift one friend can give to another is prayer. To those who knew him well it was obvious that he took prayer for others very seriously. He also made his convictions about prayer as a gift tangible by publishing a book of prayers (*Prayers for Today*, New York, NY: The Macmillan Company, 1971) which he distributed to many friends.

The original edition of this book contained prayers for many occasions, especially situations of joy and sorrow, of comfort and bereavement. These prayers address the ordinary needs of life when we must turn with confidence to God. Cardinal Cooke was one of the old fashioned Catholics who loved and used a prayer book. He wanted to share this prayer book with others. Even the simplest and best known prayers are included, no doubt more for meditation than for any other reason. In compiling the first edition Cardinal Cooke was assisted by three close friends — Monsignor James Wilders, Monsignor Charles McManus and Monsignor James Rigney. Almost all of the original prayers are in Cardinal Cooke's own words. He loved prayers for special groups of people like nurses, civil servants and teachers, and for those with special needs like the sick and the dying.

Anyone reviewing this prayer book will be struck by the universality of his concern reflecting his essentially positive attitude for all people, whom he really saw as God's children. Those who use this prayer book thoughtfully will get to know Cardinal Cooke better. One who uses it regularly for prayer will learn to pray with a more generous heart.

This second edition has been carefully revised and brought up to date by Sister Aloysius McBride, O.Carm. of the

Cardinal Cooke Guild, and by Brother Aloysius Milella, SSP and Father Edmund C. Lane, SSP of Alba House.

Certain sections, like prayer in the liturgy, have been omitted since they are no longer necessary for participation in the Mass. The editors also updated the language and citations of Sacred Scripture and have included some prayers which Cardinal Cooke composed after the publication of the original edition.

It is my hope, as Promoter of the Cause of the Beatification of Cardinal Cooke, that this little prayer book will contribute to a more widespread knowledge of this gentle and saintly man. *Benedict J. Groeschel, CFR*

PRAYER FOR THE CAUSE OF CANONIZATION OF TERENCE CARDINAL COOKE

Almighty and eternal Father, we thank you
for the exemplary life and gentle kindness of your son and
bishop, Terence Cooke. If it be your gracious will, grant
that the virtues of your servant may be recognized and
provide
a lasting example for your people.
We pray through our Lord Jesus Christ your Son who
lives and reigns with you and the Holy Spirit, one God,
for ever and ever. Amen.

Contents

PART 1

PRAYERS FOR VARIOUS INTENTIONS

FIAT VOLUNTAS TUA

PRAYERS FOR ALL PEOPLE
EVERYWHERE

FOR EVERYONE

Through him both of us have access in one Spirit to the Father. So then you are no longer strangers and aliens, but you are citizens with the saints and also members of the household of God. *(Ephesians 2:18-19)*

Father in heaven, you are the source of all love and of all life. Receive with kindness the prayers of your children on earth. Enlighten our minds in the search for truth, and direct our hearts to the love of our brothers and sisters everywhere. May we profitably employ your gifts to us so that we may one day join your family in heaven.

FOR HUMAN RIGHTS

Have we not all one father?
> Has not one God created us?
Why then are we faithless to one another,
> profaning the covenant of our ancestors?
>> *(Malachi 2:10)*

Heavenly Father, the greatest gift of freedom is the right to be one's true self; but true freedom is where peace through justice prevails.

You intended the world to furnish all individuals with the means of livelihood and the instruments of their progress as persons and members of the human family here on earth.

In these days many prejudices and mass evils scar the tissue of our common life. There are still multitudes of impoverished men, women and children who are forced to forget their inherent dignity or to give up efforts to secure recognition of their rights by others. As individuals in the economic and political communities, O Lord, they are made to count for nothing, subject to forces which deny them the power to develop their potential. These brothers and sisters of ours never become all that they might be — reflecting your glory in their freedom.

Listen to their silence, O Lord, and grant us the courage fearlessly to fight against evil and to make no peace with oppression; may we reverently use our freedom, employing it in the pursuit of justice and right among all peoples and nations to the glory of your most holy name. Amen.

FOR PEACE

Pursue peace with everyone, and the holiness without which no one will see the Lord. *(Hebrews 12:14)*

O God, source of all holy desires, right counsels, and just works, grant your servants that peace which the world cannot give, so that we may be obedient to your commands, and under your protection enjoy peace in our days and freedom from fear of our enemies.

> Lord, make me a channel of your peace.
>   Where there is hatred,
>   let me bring your love;
>   Where there is injury,
>   your pardon, Lord;
>   And where there's doubt,
>   true faith in you;

Where there's despair in life,
  let me bring hope;
Where there is darkness,
  only light;
And where there's sadness,
  ever joy.

O Master,
  grant that I may never seek
    so much to be consoled
  as to console,
to be understood
  as to understand,
to be loved,
  as to love with all my soul.
For it is in pardoning
  that we are pardoned,
in giving of ourselves
  that we receive,
and in dying
that we're born to eternal life.

                              (St. Francis of Assisi)

FOR SOCIAL JUSTICE

Whoever pursues righteousness and kindness will find life
and honor.   *(Proverbs 21:21)*

Almighty and eternal God, may your grace enkindle in
everyone a love for the many unfortunate people whom
poverty and misery reduce to a condition of life unworthy of
human beings. Arouse in the hearts of those who call you
Father a hunger and thirst for social justice, and for fraternal

love in deed and in truth. Grant, O Lord, peace in our days, peace to souls, peace to families, peace to our country, and peace among nations. Amen. *(Pope Pius XII)*

FOR JUSTICE AND PEACE

Blessed are the peacemakers, for they shall be called children of God. *(Matthew 5:9)*

O God, our Father, you have set us over all the works of your hands. You have shared with us your creative power to build a world of peace and justice — a world in which everyone can live as brothers and sisters endowed with human dignity as members of your human family.

O God, our Father, bestow on us who live in this age of space a share in your vision. Grant that we, who have seen battlefields where we have sought to destroy one another and ghettos where many of us live without dignity or hope, may now look to the stars and see our world, as the astronauts did, as "small and blue and beautiful in the eternal silence in which it floats." Grant that we, who witness millions of homeless, hungry children in a world of unparalleled scientific achievements, may enjoy the prophetic vision which sees all the members of your human family as "riders on the earth together," brothers and sisters on "that bright loveliness in the eternal cold."

O God, our Father, inspire us with faith to believe that this vision of our earth can be fulfilled. Grant us the grace to believe firmly that you have given us sufficient resources for this purpose. Show us how to use them generously to provide food, decent shelter, education, and meaningful employment for all in your family.

O God, our Father, strengthen us with humility and wisdom. Teach us to be thankful for the precious mystery of life that you have made ours. Bless our efforts to promote the total development of each and every human being that all might reach the fullness of their potential and dignity as your sons and daughters. Amen.

FOR COMMUNICATIONS AMONG ALL PEOPLES

Bear one another's burdens, and in this way you will fulfill the law of Christ. *(Galatians 6:2)*

O God, Lord of all kindness, Giver of every perfect gift, grant that the marvelous means of communication in our world — the press, radio, television and motion pictures — may advance the spiritual and material progress of all peoples.

Grant that through the news media the word of truth entrusted to the Church may further the progress of nations and the enlightenment of individuals.

Grant that the communications media may help in the struggle against ignorance and hunger, contribute toward the elimination of selfishness, and alert all hearts to the needs and legitimate aspirations of people everywhere.

Grant that by spreading understanding and respect for true human dignity, these media may help to improve the lot of all, spiritually and intellectually, thus directing them to their true destiny.

Grant that the press, radio, television, and motion pictures may teach love of virtue, self-control, the spirit of sacrifice, and attachment to freedom and peace.

Grant that individuals and nations may use the discoveries of human progress to further the advance of the world toward the one and true God.

FOR CIVIC RESPONSIBILITY

Learn to do good; seek justice, rescue the oppressed, defend the orphan, plead for the widow.   *(Isaiah 1:17)*

Heavenly Father, I have often turned away from the needs of others through my own selfishness. I have failed to fulfill your hopes for me because of my unfaithfulness. Through your mercy I ask that I may regain what I have lost through my carelessness and folly. I hope that all others may regain what they have lost through my sins of omission. I hereby pledge to assist social and civic programs that strive for the improvement of living conditions and the elimination of my neighbors' suffering, I will support all just authority, resist violence, and use all moral means to exercise the talents you have given me to aid others. Bestow your blessings on all our civil officials so that they may complete their duties justly and wisely. Amen.

FOR THE PRESIDENT AND
OTHER CIVIL AUTHORITIES

The spirit of the LORD shall rest on him,
    the spirit of wisdom and understanding,

the spirit of counsel and might,
    the spirit of knowledge and the fear of the LORD.
    His delight shall be in the fear of the LORD.
He shall not judge by what his eyes see,
    or decide by what his ears hear;
but with righteousness he shall judge the poor,
    and decide with equity for the meek of the earth.

(Isaiah 11:2-4)

We pray you, O God of wisdom and justice, to assist with your Holy Spirit of counsel and fortitude the President. May his administration be conducted in righteousness, and may he encourage due respect for virtue and religion, a faithful execution of the laws in justice and mercy, and the restraint of vice and immorality. Let the light of your wisdom direct the deliberations of Congress and shine forth in all laws framed for our rule and government. May they tend to the preservation of peace, the promotion of national happiness, the increase of industry and knowledge, and the blessings of equal liberty.

We recommend to your mercy all our fellow citizens, that they may be blessed in the knowledge, and sanctified in the observance, of your most holy law; that they may be preserved in union, and in that peace which the world cannot give; and after enjoying the blessings of this life, that they be admitted to those which are eternal. Amen.

FOR THE RIGHT TO LIFE

"You've heard that it was said to the ancients, You shall not murder, and that whoever does commit murder shall be liable to judgment." *(Matthew 5:21)*

O heavenly Father, strengthen us against the mounting forces of anti-life; enlighten those who walk in this deadly way that they may see the enormity of their sin and return to the generous observance of the divine law. We pray, too, for mothers, that they may prize the great privilege of motherhood; and that they may bring up their children in the holy love and fear of God, thus saving their own immortal souls and furthering the honor and glory of their Maker. Through Christ, our Lord. Amen.

Pray for us, St. Gerard, protector of the mother and her unborn child, that we may be worthy of the promises of Christ!

FOR LOVERS OF EARTH

When I look at your heavens,
        the work of your fingers,
    the moon and the stars that
        you have established;
    what are human beings that you
        are mindful of them,
    mortals that you care for them?
Yet you have made them a little lower than God
    and crowned them with glory and honor.
You have given them dominion
        over the works of your hands;
    you have put all things under their feet,
all sheep and oxen,
    and also the beasts of the field,
the birds of the air, and the fish of the sea,
    whatever passes along the paths of the seas.

(Psalm 8:3-9)

Be praised, my Lord, with all your creatures,
    especially Sir Brother Sun,
        by whom you give us the light of day!
How beautiful and radiant he is, and with great splendor.
    Of you, Most High, he is a symbol!
Be praised, my Lord, for Sister Moon and the Stars!
    In the sky you formed them, bright and lovely
            and fair.
Be praised, my Lord, for Brother Wind,

and for the Air, and cloudy and clear and all Weather,
    by which you give sustenance to your creatures!
Be praised, my Lord, for Sister Water,
    who is very useful and humble and lovely and chaste!
Be praised, my Lord, for Brother Fire,
    by whom you give us light at night;
      he is beautiful and merry and mighty and strong.
Be praised, my Lord, for our Sister, Mother Earth,
    who sustains and governs us,
      and produces fruits with colorful flowers and
        leaves!   *(St. Francis of Assisi)*

FOR TRAVELERS

The LORD went in front of them in a pillar of cloud by day,
to lead them along the way, and in a pillar of fire by night, to
give them light, so that they might travel by day and by night.
Neither the pillar of cloud by day nor the pillar of fire by night
left its place in front of the people.   *(Exodus 13:21-22)*

O God, you have given us a rough road to travel, but you have
not left us alone. You guided our father Abraham through a
sun-blazed and scorching desert to a land that was his only in
promise, a land that he could lay claim to only by faith.

You led your Chosen People, the forerunners of your Church,
away from a slave country to the land of promise, a land
whose enjoyment was not easily won, whose fulfillment
demanded the rigorous exercise of justice, the dangerous
pursuit of freedom.

You sent your only Son, Jesus Christ, accompanied by dimly
comprehending followers, on the road to Jerusalem, where
he dashed their hopes for an earthly kingdom by dying as a

criminal on a cross. In his resurrection and glory is our only pledge of life.

May your Spirit move in us as we depart on our journeys to familiar places of work or study, to unknown regions of conflict or danger, to visit the sick, to seek needed relaxation. May he direct us in our quest for meaning, peace, and love. May your Spirit breathe into us an effective desire to serve all whom we meet on our way to our eternal encounter with you.

Strengthen us. Fill our eyes with hope, and our hearts with loving concern for our neighbor. Raise us up if we fall. Urge us on if we are tempted to stop, and welcome us at journey's end with the fatherly embrace that you have reserved for all who faithfully seek to do your holy will.

FROM THE UNIQUE PERSPECTIVE
OF OUTER SPACE

When I look at your heavens,
the work of your fingers,
the moon and the stars that
you have established...
O LORD, our Sovereign,
how majestic is your name
in all the earth! *(Psalm 8:3, 10)*

O God, the beauties of the universe are but pale reflections of your glory. The vast reaches of space dimly mirror your infinite timelessness. The intricate design of the planets, stars, and galaxies is a shadowy illustration of your all-embracing wisdom.

You have given us a home, one tiny sphere among the millions that have come forth from your hand. You have given us knowledge and a thirst to reach out for new frontiers. You have given us a restlessness that can be fully satisfied only by you.

Astronauts have walked on the moon. One day they may walk on other worlds. May the view of our little planet, seen from the lifeless surface of the moon, heighten our awareness of how fragile is our grasp of this earth.

May we be forcefully reminded that in your Son we are brothers and sisters of a common Father. May we realize that your Spirit binds us together in love, if only we accept his invitation.

Finally, may we take renewed courage in committing ourselves to the great challenge of transforming this world into a Kingdom where your love reigns supreme.

PRAYERS FOR THE CHURCH

FOR THE CHURCH

So he came and proclaimed peace to you who were far off and peace to those who were near; for through him both of us have access in one Spirit to the Father. So then you are no longer strangers and aliens, but you are citizens with the saints and also members of the household of God, built upon the foundation of the apostles and prophets, with Christ Jesus himself as the cornerstone. In him the whole structure is joined together and grows into a holy temple in the Lord; in whom you also are built together spiritually into a dwelling place for God. *(Ephesians 2:17-22)*

Father in heaven, mercifully assist your Church, and by your heavenly power establish her as the temple of your Spirit. May the love and grace of the Holy Spirit renew your anointed servants, that they may glorify their Father and Jesus Christ, their brother and Lord. Amen.

FOR ALL THE PEOPLE OF GOD

But you are "a chosen race, a royal priesthood, a holy nation, God's own people, in order that you may proclaim the mighty acts" of him who called you out of darkness into his marvelous light.

> Once you were not a people,
> but now you are God's people;
>
> once you had not received mercy,
> but now you have received mercy.
>
> *(1 Peter 2:9-10)*

Almighty and eternal Father, shower your blessings on all of us, the people you claim as your own. Instill in our hearts an unwavering love for you. Help us to keep your commandments, to walk in your paths, and to acquire the fullness of the gift of loving you and each other. Help us to meditate on the sufferings of your divine Son, so that we may learn from his example to bear our troubles with patience.

Grant us that true humility exemplified by your Son, so that we may never provoke you to anger by pride, but rather move you by our humility to grant us your help. Take out of our hearts all sinful desires and all worldly ambition, so that we may live temperate, honest, and devout lives, and work together for your glory, for the good of all the world and for a lasting peace on earth. Then, at this life's end, may we attain together the reward of life forever in heaven.

FOR UNITY WITHIN THE CHURCH

"But I'm praying not only for them
  but also for those who believe in me
    through their word,...
And I made Your name known to them
  and I'll make it known,
That the love with which You have loved me
  may be in them,
    and I in them."   *(John 17:20, 26)*

O Lord, make us ever mindful of the words of your servant Augustine: "In essentials, unity; in non-essentials, liberty; in all things, charity." Strengthen the members of your Church so that they may prayerfully apply these words in all their thoughts and deeds. Amen.

FOR CHRISTIAN UNITY

And I have other sheep who are not
   of this fold,
I must lead them,
   and they'll listen to my voice,
      and become one flock, one shepherd.

(John 10:16)

O God, the Father of our Savior, Jesus Christ, give us the grace seriously to take to heart the great dangers we are in by our unhappy divisions. Remove from us all hatred and prejudice and whatever else may keep us from union and concord. As there is but one Body and one Spirit, one hope of our calling, one Lord, one faith, one baptism, one God and Father of us all, so may we all be of one heart and of one soul, united in one holy bond of truth and peace, of faith and charity. May we together glorify you through Christ our Lord. Amen.

FOR THE VITALITY OF THE CHURCH

May God be gracious to us and bless us
   and make his face to shine upon us,
that your way may be known upon earth,
   your saving power among all nations.
Let the peoples praise you, O God;
   let all the peoples praise you.

Let the nations be glad and sing for joy,
   for you judge the peoples with equity
   and guide the nations upon earth.
Let the peoples praise you, O God;
   let all the peoples praise you.

The earth has yielded its increase;
  God, our God, has blessed us.
May God continue to bless us;
  let all the ends of the earth revere him.

(Psalm 67:2-8)

O Savior, who shed your own blood to reconcile earth and heaven, by your grace strengthen the Church, the living witness of the faith. All-merciful Lord, let her mission of salvation be as wide as the world.

FOR THE MISSIONARY CHURCH

Go, therefore, and make disciples of all nations, baptizing them in the name of the Father and of the Son and of the Holy Spirit, and teach them to observe all that I've commanded you. Know that I'll be with you all the days until the end of the age." (Matthew 28:19-20)

O God, you desire that all people should be saved and come to the knowledge of your truth. Therefore, send, we beg you, laborers into your harvest, and grant them grace to speak your word with all trust, that your words may be heard and glorified, and that all nations may know you, the one true God, and him whom you have sent, Jesus Christ your Son, our Lord who, with you, lives and reigns, world without end. Amen.

TO MARY, MOTHER OF THE CHURCH

And when he came into her presence he said, "Hail, full of grace, the Lord is with you!" Now she was perplexed by this saying and wondered what sort of greeting this could be. And the angel said to her,

"Fear not, Mary —
      you have found grace before the Lord.
And, behold, you will conceive in your womb
            and will bear a son,
      and you shall name him Jesus.
He'll be great and will be called
            Son of the Most High,
      and the Lord God will give him the throne
            of his father, David,
And he'll reign over the house of Jacob forever,
      and his kingdom will have no end."   *(Luke 1:28-33)*

THE MEMORARE

Remember, O most compassionate Virgin Mary, that never was it known that anyone who fled to your protection, implored your help, or sought your intercession, was left unaided. Inspired by this confidence we fly unto you, O Virgin of virgins, our Mother; to you do we come, before you we kneel, sinful and sorrowful. O Mother of the Word Incarnate, despise not our petitions in our necessities, but in your mercy hear and answer them. Amen.

TO ST. PETER AND ST. PAUL

And he said to them, "Go into the whole world and proclaim the good news to all creation. Whoever believes and is baptized will be saved, but whoever doesn't believe will be condemned.   (Mark 16:15-16)

To St. Peter

Glorious St. Peter, in reward for your generous faith, your sincere humility and burning love, you were honored by Jesus Christ with the leadership of the other apostles and the primacy of the whole Church, of which you were made the foundation stone. Obtain for us the grace of lively faith that shall not fear to profess itself openly, fully, and in all its manifestations, even to the giving of blood and life should occasion demand it. May we sacrifice life itself rather than deny our faith. Obtain for us also a sincere attachment to our Holy Mother the Church.

Grant that we may ever keep sincerely and closely united to the Holy Father who is the heir of your authority, and the true, visible head of the Catholic Church. Grant that we may follow the teaching and counsels of the Church. May we be obedient to all her precepts so as to enjoy peace here on earth, and to attain one day eternal happiness in heaven.

To St. Paul

Glorious St. Paul, from being a persecutor of the Christian name, you became its most zealous apostle. To make Jesus, our Divine Savior, known to the uttermost parts of the earth, you suffered prison, scourging, stoning, shipwreck, and all manner of persecution, and shed the last drop of your blood. Obtain for us the grace to accept the infirmities, sufferings, and misfortunes of this life as favors of the divine mercy. So may we never grow weary of the trials of our exile, but rather show ourselves ever more faithful and fervent. Amen.

TO ST. MICHAEL THE ARCHANGEL

Then I looked, and I heard the voice of many angels surrounding the throne and the living creature and the elders; they numbered myriads of myriads and thousands of thousands, singing with full voice,

"Worthy is the Lamb that was slaughtered
to receive power and wealth and wisdom and might
and honor and glory and blessing!"

(Revelation 5:11-12)

St. Michael the Archangel, defend us in battle; be our safeguard against the malice and snares of the devil. May God restrain him, we humbly pray, and do you, O Prince of the heavenly host, by the divine power, thrust into hell Satan and the other evil spirits who go about the world seeking the ruin of souls. Amen.

FOR THE HOLY FATHER AND THE BISHOPS

And now I tell you, that you are Peter,
And on this rock I will build my church,
And the gates of hell will not prevail
against it.
I will give you the keys of the Kingdom
of Heaven,
And whatever you bind on earth will have been
bound in the heavens,
And whatever you loose on earth will have been
loosed in the heavens." *(Matthew 16:18-19)*

For the Pope

O God, shepherd and ruler of all the faithful, look down favorably upon your servant whom you have been pleased to appoint pastor over your Church. Grant, we beseech you, that he may benefit both by word and example those over whom he is set, and thus attain eternal life together with the flock committed to his care. Through Christ our Lord. Amen.

Almighty, everlasting God, have mercy upon our Sovereign Pontiff, and direct him according to your clemency into the way of everlasting salvation; that by your grace, he may desire those things that are pleasing to you and perform them with all his strength. Through Christ our Lord. Amen.

For the Bishops

"Keep watch over yourselves and over all the flock, of which the Holy Spirit has made you overseers, to shepherd the church of God that he obtained with the blood of his own Son." *(Acts 20:28)*

O God, shepherd and ruler of all the faithful, look with favor upon the bishops whom you have been pleased to appoint pastors of the Church. Grant, we beseech you, that by both word and example they may edify those over whom they are placed, and together with the flocks committed to their care, may attain unto life everlasting. Through Christ our Lord. Amen.

For Priests

In the presence of God and of Christ Jesus, who is to judge the living and the dead, and in view of his appearing and his kingdom, I solemnly urge you:

proclaim the message; be persistent whether the time is favorable or unfavorable; convince, rebuke, and encourage with the utmost patience in teaching. As for you, always be sober, endure suffering, do the work of an evangelist, carry out your ministry fully.
(2 Timothy 4:1-2, 5)

O Jesus, you desire that we pray the Lord of the harvest to send zealous laborers into his harvest. In your mercy raise up in your Church, and especially in this diocese, numerous and holy priests, who will take your divine heart as their model and in the exercise of their holy priesthood promote the glory of your heavenly Father and the salvation of those souls whom you have redeemed with your precious blood. Amen.

O Mary, Mother of God and Mother of the first and eternal Priest of the Most High, increase the number of those who share in his priesthood and in his power, and continue the holy mission of your divine Son in the whole world and especially in our own country. Amen.

FOR BROTHERS AND SISTERS

We have gifts that differ according to the grace given to us: prophecy, in proportion to faith; ministry, in ministering; the teacher, in teaching; the exhorter, in exhortation; the giver, in generosity; the leader, in diligence; the compassionate, in cheerfulness. *(Romans 12:6-8)*

FOR BROTHERS

Our Father, we offer this prayer on behalf of the Brothers who serve your Church, the people of God, through the special dedication of their lives. We pray that their dedication will grow in courage and flexibility to meet the ever-growing and ever-changing needs of the Church in our day. We pray that they will face the future with the clear vision of men who are open to the prompting of the Holy Spirit, ever aware that your grace renews and strengthens their every effort.

Finally, we pray that in every apostolate to which their dedication leads them, they may always realize the enormous contribution of their life service, so well summarized by the Second Vatican Council: "A life consecrated by a profession of the evangelical counsels is one of surpassing value."

Father, we submit our petitions in the name of your Son, our Lord Jesus Christ, whose gospel we strive to live. Amen.

For Sisters

Our Father, we offer this prayer in thanksgiving for Sisters, whose unique role of consecrated dedication to the Church is so in keeping with their fulfillment as Christian witnesses and Christian women. We rejoice in their courage and vision, manifested by their efforts to express religious community as an answer to the special needs of your Church today. We pray that they will have the clarity of vision and the courage of conviction to be open to the workings of the Holy Spirit, so that their lives will express a spirit of living prayer and the power of true Christian witness. We ask that by their leadership they will be looked on as symbols of hope in a world which is uncertain and troubled.

Finally, we pray that they will be heartened by the living presence of Christ, in whom "we live and move and have our being," so that their lives will be a unique testimony to the value of religious community in the pilgrim Church. Amen.

FOR VOCATIONS TO THE PRIESTHOOD AND THE RELIGIOUS LIFE

Then he said to his disciples,

> "The harvest is plentiful,
> But the laborers are few;

so implore the Lord of the harvest to send out laborers to his harvest." *(Matthew 9:37-38)*

Lord Jesus Christ, Savior of the world! We humbly beg you to manifest in your Church the Spirit whom you so abundantly bestowed upon your apostles. Call, we pray you, very many to your priesthood and to the religious life. And may zeal for your glory and the salvation of souls inflame these whom you have chosen. By your Spirit strengthen them, that they may be saints in your likeness. Amen.

Stir up in your Church, O Lord, the devotion and fortitude needed to make worthy ministers for your altar and powerful preachers of your word. In your kindness be attentive to our prayers and offerings that the stewards of your mysteries may increase in number and persevere to the end in loving you. Grant that those whom you have chosen as ministers of the redemption may, with pure minds, be worthy servants of your boundless love. Amen.

PRAYERS FOR FAMILY AND FRIENDS

ON THE OCCASION OF BAPTISM

Do you not know that all of us who have been baptized into Christ Jesus were baptized into his death? Therefore we have been buried with him by baptism into death, so that, just as Christ was raised from the dead by the glory of the Father, so we too might walk in newness of life. *(Romans 6:3-4)*

Heavenly Father, the water with which you cover so much of the earth can be gentle in a summer rain, or powerful in a mighty river. In baptism you use water to signify and accomplish the spiritual rebirth of your children.

The Spirit which brooded over the waters of creation breathes his presence into souls with the saving action of the waters of the Red Sea, the refreshment of the water struck from the rock in the desert, and the fulfillment of what was symbolized by the baptism of John in the Jordan.

May those who are baptized this day be born again in water and through the Holy Spirit to a long life as children of God and co-heirs with Christ for ever and ever. Amen.

FAMILY PRAYERS

Husbands, love your wives and never treat them harshly. Children, obey your parents in everything, for this is your acceptable duty in the Lord. Fathers, do not provoke your children, or they may lose heart. *(Colossians 3:19-21)*

O merciful God! We humbly beseech you to send your blessing continuously upon us, and to make us thankful for all that you have given us. As you have made us one in the grace of matrimony, grant that we may also inwardly be of one heart and of one mind, paying due honor to each other, united in love to you, and to each other in you. Grant, too, that we may live together in peace and holiness as faithful members of your Church, denying ourselves and being of mutual help, comfort, and support to each other all the days of our lives.

Give us grace to train our children in your faith and love. Bless us with health and strength, if it be your will, and with whatever else your good providence shall see to be best for our souls and bodies. Do prepare us day by day for our departure from this life, that together we may inherit eternal life in your heavenly kingdom. Through the merits of Jesus Christ, our Lord and Savior. Amen.

Parents' Prayer for Children

O Lord God! You have called us to the holy state of matrimony and have been pleased to render our union fruitful. You have made us glad in the sublime state of life wherein you have placed us by a certain likeness to your own infinite fruitfulness. We heartily recommend to you our dear children, and entrust them to your fatherly care and all-powerful protection, that they may grow daily in your holy fear. May they lead perfect Christian lives and be a source of consolation, not only to us who have shared with you in giving them life, but also, and chiefly, to you who are their Creator.

Behold, O Lord, in what a world they must live! Be watchful; help and defend them.

Grant us the grace to guide them in the paths of virtue and in the way of your commandments. This we will do by the right pattern of our own life and practice, by our perfect observance of your holy law and that of our Holy Mother Church. In order that we may do so faithfully, make us conscious of our graces and our obligations. Nevertheless, all our efforts will be unavailing unless you, O almighty and merciful God, shall make them fruitful by your heavenly blessings. Amen.

For One's Family

O Jesus, our Lord and our brother! We commend our family and all that is ours to your protection; we confide all to your love. Fill our house with blessings, even as you filled the holy house of Nazareth with your presence; before all else, keep sin far from it. Do you alone reign by your law, by your most holy love, and by the exercise of every Christian virtue. Let all of us obey you, love you and study how to copy in our own lives your example, that of Mary your Mother, and that of your blameless guardian, St. Joseph.

Keep all evils and misfortunes far from us and our house, but grant that we may be ever in harmony with your divine will, even in the sorrows which you send to us. Finally, grant us the grace to live in perfect harmony and in the fullness of charity toward our neighbor. Grant that every one of us may deserve by a holy life the comfort of your holy sacraments at the hour of death. Amen.

ACT OF CONSECRATION TO THE HOLY FAMILY

O Jesus, our most loving Redeemer! You came to enlighten the world with your teaching and example, and to live the greater part of your life with Mary and Joseph in their home at Nazareth. Thus you sanctified the family that was to be an example to all Christian families. Graciously receive our family, which is dedicated and consecrated to you this day. Protect it; guard it and establish it in holy fear, in peace, and in the harmony of Christian charity. By conforming ourselves to the model of your family, may we all without exception attain to eternal happiness.

Mary, Mother of Jesus and our Mother! By your intercession make this, our humble offering, acceptable to Jesus and obtain for us his grace and blessings. O St. Joseph, most holy guardian of Jesus and Mary! Assist us by your prayers in all our spiritual and temporal needs, so that we may be able to praise our Divine Savior, Jesus, together with Mary and you for all eternity. Amen.

FOR YOUTH

For this reason, since the day we heard it, we have not ceased praying for you and asking that you may be filled with the knowledge of God's will in all spiritual wisdom and understanding, so that you may lead lives worthy of the Lord, fully pleasing to him, as you bear fruit in every good work and as you grow in the knowledge of God. May you be made strong with all the strength that comes from his glorious power, and may you be prepared to endure everything with patience, while joyfully giving thanks to the Father, who has enabled you to share in the inheritance of the saints in the light. He has rescued us from the power of darkness and transferred us into the kingdom of his beloved Son, in whom we have redemption, the forgiveness of sins.   *(Colossians 1:9-13)*

FOR CHARACTER

O Lord Jesus Christ, who during your childhood became the model of all young people, guide us along the path of youth. Give us the generosity to love others, the character to be truthful and honest, the discipline to obey our parents, the wisdom to know what is right, and the courage to do it. Let us always use our influence to make others good, and never let us follow anyone who does not follow you. Amen.

FOR WISDOM

Dear Lord, let us grow daily in wisdom, age, and grace. This was the gospel formula for the young Christ, it must be the gospel formula for us all. Christ grew till he stood a man — obedient to God his Father, king of all his people, one with his chosen apostles, as he was to be one always with those who choose him for their Lord and guide. We are young people. We are eager for truth and justice. Let both prevail. We shall grow older. Let this growth be in faith, in charity, and in understanding until we shall all be united with you forever. Amen.

Come Holy Spirit, giver of light and love, strengthen me in the knowledge of God our Father and Redeemer. Enlighten and sanctify me in my youth and throughout my life, so that through Christ in the Holy Eucharist I may know, love, and serve you in all things. Author of wisdom and holiness, give me the grace to know and to overcome the temptations which befall me. Help me to teach those who do not know you, and to aid those who preach your doctrine. Blessed light of life, instill in my heart a desire to know the truth, to embrace it faithfully throughout my life, and in so doing enjoy peace in this world and everlasting happiness with you in heaven. Amen.

For Courage

O Almighty God, let the brightness of your glory shine upon us, so that the Holy Spirit, light of your light, may strengthen the hearts of those who are reborn through your grace. Help us to see our duty clearly and fulfill it courageously for your honor and glory. Amen.

FOR CHOOSING A STATE OF LIFE

Now there are varieties of gifts, but the same Spirit; and there are varieties of services, but the same Lord. All these are activated by one and the same Spirit, who allots to each one individually just as the Spirit chooses.

(1 Corinthians 12:4-5, 11)

My heavenly Father, I sincerely wish to dedicate my whole life to you, to please you in everything I do, and to guide my life by your will.

I realize, Father, that you wish me to use the freedom you have given me. I am deeply concerned about my free choice of the state of life in which I can live most happily and serve you best. Guide me in my choice, O Lord, and help me to decide wisely. Give me also the strength to persevere in following my decision. I ask this grace through Jesus Christ your Son, who perfectly knew and fulfilled your will for him.

ON THE OCCASION OF A MARRIAGE

"For this reason a man will leave his father and mother and be joined to his wife, and the two will become one flesh."

(Ephesians 5:31)

Heavenly Father, you created us in your own image and likeness, and re-created us through grace as your children.

At the same time you re-created the union of man and woman in sacramental marriage into a living image of the union of Christ with those who are his members, his body.

Give to those who have entered this common life today an awareness of the holiness and strength of their union as they carry the message of Christ's love for his members, and the inseparable bond which his bride, his body, has with him.

With faith in you and in each other, may their lives bear witness to your love and theirs, and may their love last like yours into eternity. Amen.

FOR A HAPPY MARRIED LIFE

And the rib that the LORD God had taken from the man he made into a woman and brought her to the man. Then the man said,

"This at last is bone of my bones
   and flesh of my flesh;
this one shall be called
   Woman,
for out of Man this one was
   taken."

Therefore a man leaves his father and his mother and clings to his wife, and they become one flesh. *(Gn 2:22-24)*

Father in heaven, we your children remember so vividly the day we were united in marriage before your altar. Give us your blessing each day, and strengthen our love for each other so that we may serve you in steadfastness and peace.

FOR MOTHERS

Happy is everyone who fears the LORD,
   who walks in his ways.
You shall eat the fruit of the
     labor of your hands;
  you shall be happy, and it
     shall go well with you.
Your wife will be like a fruitful vine
     within your house;
  your children will be like olive shoots
     around your table.
Thus shall the man be blessed
  who fears the LORD.
The LORD bless you from Zion.
  May you see the prosperity of Jerusalem
     all the days of your life.
May you see your children's children,
  Peace be upon Israel! *(Psalm 128:1-6)*

St. Monica, Patroness of Mothers

Blessed Monica, mother of St. Augustine, our Father in heaven looked with mercy upon your tears. Your son's conversion and heroic sanctification were the fruit of your prayers. From your heavenly home, happy mother of a saint, pray for those who wander far from God, and add your prayers to those of all mothers who worry over their sons and daughters. Pray for us that, following your example, we may in the company of our children at length enjoy the eternal vision of our Father in heaven. Amen.

To St. Gerard, Patron of Expectant Mothers

St. Gerard, powerful intercessor before God and wonder-worker of our day, I call upon you and seek your aid. You, who on earth always fulfilled God's designs, help me do the holy will of God. Beseech the Master of Life, from whom all parenthood proceeds, that I may raise up children to God in this life and heirs to the kingdom of his glory in the world to come. Amen.

FOR THE AGING

You shall rise before the aged, and defer to the old; and you shall fear your God: I am the LORD.   *(Leviticus 19:32)*

Lord, you know better than I myself that I am not getting any younger and will some day be old. Keep me from getting too talkative, and particularly keep me from the fatal habit of thinking that I must say something on every subject and on every occasion.

Release me from craving to straighten out everybody's affairs.

Make me thoughtful, but not moody; helpful, but not bossy. With my vast store of wisdom it seems a pity not to use it all, but you know, Lord, that I want a few friends at the end.

Keep my mind free from the recitals of endless details; give wings to my words that they may fly directly to the point. Teach me the glorious lesson that occasionally I may be mistaken... a sour individual is one of the crowning works of the devil.

Help me to extract all possible fun out of life. There are so many funny things around us and I don't want to miss any of them.

Dear Lord, as I grow older do not let me ever be fearful or lose hope. Help me to see the good around me rather than the evil, and give me grace and strength to continue to love and serve you until the last breath of life. Then when my task is ended and the day is over, lead me to the peace and joy of heaven to be with you and all my loved ones forever. Amen.

TO MY GUARDIAN ANGEL

But the angel of the Lord came down into the furnace beside Azariah and his companions. He drove the flames of the fire outside the furnace while, in the middle of the furnace, he blew upon them a cool, dew-laden breeze, so that the fire did not touch them or cause them pain or trouble.

(Daniel 3:49-50)

Angel of God, my guardian dear,
To whom his love commits me here;
Ever this day be at my side,
To light and guard, to rule and guide. Amen.

FOR THE DECEASED

He also took up a collection, man by man, to the amount of two thousand drachmas of silver, and sent it to Jerusalem to provide for a sin offering. In doing this he acted very well and honorably, taking account of the resurrection. For if he were not expecting that those who had fallen would rise again, it would have been superfluous and foolish to pray for the dead. But if he was looking to the splendid reward that is laid up for those who fall asleep in godliness, it was a holy and pious thought. Therefore he made atonement for the dead, so that they might be delivered from their sin.

(2 Maccabees 12:43-45)

FOR DECEASED FAMILY AND FRIENDS

O Heavenly Father, have pity on my deceased friends and relatives. Through your infinite mercy and goodness raise them to everlasting joy and speedy union with you. To them and to all who rest in Christ, grant happiness, light, and heavenly peace. Amen.

UPON THE DEATH OF A DEAR ONE

We seem to give them back to you, O God, who first gave them to us. Yet as you did not lose them in giving, so do we not lose them by their return. Not as the world gives, do you give. What you give you do not take away, for what is yours is ours also if we are yours. And life is eternal, and love is immortal, and death is only a horizon; and a horizon is nothing save the limit of our sight.

Lift us up, strong Son of God, that we may see further. Remove the scales from our eyes that we may see more clearly; draw us closer to you that we may know ourselves to be nearer to our loved ones who are with you. And while you prepare a place for us, prepare us also for that happy place, that where you are we may also be forever. Amen.

For the Faithful Departed

O Lord God Almighty! I beseech you by the power of the precious blood, which your divine Son Jesus shed in his passion, to deliver the souls in purgatory, especially the soul which is nearest to its entrance into your glory, so that it may soon begin to praise you and bless you in heaven forever. Amen.

O Lord, the Creator and Redeemer of all the faithful, grant to the souls of your servants departed the remission of all their sins; that by the humble supplications of your Church, they may obtain that pardon which they have always desired of your mercy. Amen.

PRAYERS FOR ALL WHO LABOR

TO ST. JOSEPH

And when he came to his home town he taught them in their synagogue, with the result that they were amazed and said, "Where does this fellow get this wisdom and these mighty works? Isn't this the carpenter's son? *(Matthew 13:54-55)*

O glorious St. Joseph, model of those who are devoted to labor, obtain for me the grace to work in a spirit of penance for the expiation of my many sins; to work conscientiously, putting the call of duty above my inclinations; to work with thankfulness and joy, considering it an honor to employ and develop by means of labor the gifts received from God; to work with order, peace, moderation, and patience, never shrinking from weariness and trials; to work, above all, with purity of intention and with detachment from self, keeping unceasingly before my eyes death and the account I must give of time lost, talents unused, good omitted, and vain complacency in success, so fatal to the work of God. All for Jesus, all through Mary, all after your example, O patriarch Joseph; such shall be my watchword in life and in death. Amen.

FOR DOCTORS AND NURSES

I am going to bring [this city] recovery and healing; I will heal them and reveal to them an abundance of prosperity and peace.   *(Jeremiah 33:6)*

A Doctor's Prayer

Spirit of love, wisdom, mercy, and compassion, Holy Spirit of God! Descend upon us, we pray, as we invoke your blessings on this, our work, to your praise and glory. Enlighten our minds; enlarge our hearts; encourage our labors. Enliven our desires to glorify you by serving others in these times of trial and tribulation.

You are the Spirit of him who lovingly laid his healing hand upon the sick, who touched the eyes of the blind, who opened the ears of the deaf, who cleansed the leper, and filled souls with faith, hope and love. Trusting in your great mercies, whose number is without end, we beg your inspiration as we offer you our works and our resources in the service of those who have been and who will be affected and afflicted by sickness and disease.

A Nurse's Prayer

O wondrous angel of the Agony! You were sent by the Father to strengthen and encourage his Son as he lay prostrate in Gethsemane. Obtain for me, I beg of you, the grace to understand more clearly my sublime vocation as a Christian nurse. May I dedicate myself more intelligently, more faithfully, and more generously to my Savior, now suffering in the sick.

For Nurses

Dear Lord, model and inspiration of the nursing profession, I know that when you ascended into heaven, you left the care of your sick to those whom you have blessed with the holy vocation of nursing. Help them to be faithful to that calling so that they can always do the things you want them to do in the way that you want. Grant that their voices may be gentle; that their hands may have the soothing and sensitive touch of your hands; that their presence may bring something of the hope and consolation which your presence brought to the sufferers of your day.

They want to do all these things, dear Lord, but they know that they are weak and can do little without your aid. Please give them that aid this day and every day of their lives, that they may always be what they know you want them to be — angels in the sickroom. Amen.

FOR LAWYERS

Yet the law is holy and the commandment is holy and just and good.   *(Romans 7:12)*

O glorious martyr, St. Thomas More, your constant prayer was that your heart should never grow cold or lukewarm in love for your Savior, Jesus. Out of love for your enemies you went to your martyrdom with a kindly jest on your lips. Pray for us that we may obtain the grace which was your glory, of cheerful giving to both God and neighbor. The joy of your heart won for you many graces, for "the Lord indeed loves a cheerful giver."

From your glory on high, continue to intercede for us until we join your happy company. Pray that our joy of heart may help to lighten the hearts of the weary and depressed, and lead them to him who lovingly bids us all: "Learn of me, for I am meek and humble of heart, and you shall find rest for your souls." Amen.

FOR TEACHERS OF CHRISTIAN DOCTRINE

"The Intercessor, the Holy Spirit the Father will send in my name, will teach you everything and will remind you of all the things I told you."   *(John 14:26)*

Lord God, I go to meet them again —
Faces filled with innocence not long ago,
Faces now blank, expressionless, apathetic.
Does this mask guilt, or fear, or the failure of people like
    me?
When I speak to them, they will answer, mumbling and
    unsure.
When we pray together, the prayer will be scattered and
    halfhearted.
They will have come again unprepared, uninterested,
    unconcerned.
I ask them: "Do you deny God?"
They do not.
"Do you deny Christ?"
They do not.
"Do you deny the Church?"
They do not.
They won't deny, but they won't affirm.
They can't articulate what they don't believe any better
    than they can say what they do believe.
They haunt me, these faces and voices and refusals to deny
    or affirm.
I'd welcome honest denial —
At least I could grapple with that instead of trying to gain
    footing on slippery, filmy haze.
Lord God, let it be different today.
Whatever is wrong, let it become right.

If it is my own pride in my own learning they scorn,
    let the pride be gone.
If it is my own sin they sense,
    let them sense my sorrow, too.
If my own weakness repels them,
    show them your strength.
You live inside me.
    I know that you are there.
Sometimes barely present to my consciousness —
Just enough to make me keep going when I want to stop,
Just enough to make me stop when I want to go,
Just enough that at my coldest
    I cannot forget you.
Can't they see that?
How do I manage to hide you from them?
If they could see you in me, perhaps they wouldn't fear
    any longer
        to let me see you in them.
There isn't much time, Lord;
Soon their days of instruction will be done.
Whatever they are going to learn,
    they must learn now,
And I know they could learn it all in one flaming moment,
    if I could show them you.
I don't know how to do that; no one does.
You alone can make it happen.
So now I will go to them,
    unworthy to speak your name,
But going because, if I don't, no one will.
Speak to them through me, Lord,
    speak to them through me.

FOR TEACHERS

I pray that the God of our Lord Jesus Christ, the Father of glory, may give you a spirit of wisdom and revelation as you come to know him, so that, with the eyes of your heart enlightened, you may know what is the hope to which he has called you, what are the riches of his glorious inheritance among the saints, and what is the immeasurable greatness of his power for us who believe, according to the working of his great power. God put this power to work in Christ when he raised him from the dead and seated him at his right hand in the heavenly places, far above all rule and authority and power and dominion, and above every name that is named, not only in this age but also in the age to come. And he has put all things under his feet and has made him the head over all things for the Church, which is his body, the fullness of him who fills all in all. *(Ephesians 1:17-23)*

Heavenly Father, Creator of life and source of all knowledge, help me to be an instrument in the creation of wisdom and understanding in your world.

Divine Master, you came to teach us the most important lessons the world will ever learn; help me to teach my students with your dedication and patient love.

Holy Spirit of truth, sent to enlighten our hearts and minds, help me to see clearly the value of my role as teacher and to give my students a genuine love for the truth.

Eternal Trinity, give me the humility to accept your mystery and the courage to ponder your hidden ways; help me to build your kingdom anew in the hearts of those I teach, with the honesty to acknowledge my own shortcomings and the grace to overcome them. Through Christ our Lord. Amen.

FOR STUDENTS

"Blessed be the name of God
    from age to age,
  for wisdom and power are his.
He changes times and seasons,
  deposes kings and sets up kings;
he gives wisdom to the wise
  and knowledge to those who
      have understanding.
He reveals deep and hidden things;
  he knows what is in the darkness,
  and light dwells with him.
To you, O God of my ancestors,
  I give thanks and praise,
for you have given me wisdom and power
  and have now revealed to me
      what we asked of you,
  for you have revealed to us
      what the king commanded."

(Daniel 2:20-23)

Lord Jesus, my example and my brother, you were once a student just like me. As you learned from Mary and Joseph both the trade of the carpenter and the wonderful joys of family life, help me to learn from my parents and teachers the things I ought to know in order to live as a useful and happy human being.

Give me the perseverance to keep at my studies, knowing that I cannot really live a full life unless I master them.

Give me the honesty to realize how much I still do not know, and that all my life must be a constant search for truth.

Give me the grace to see that all I learn will be useless information unless I put it to the service of others and try to make their lives a little better by the knowledge I have made my own.

Give me the humility to accept mysteries I cannot understand and the courage to live my life in the light of a gospel which the world finds foolish.

Lord Jesus, once a student just like me, help me to learn to be more and more like you. Amen.

FOR WORKERS

The LORD God took the man and put him in the garden of Eden to till it and keep it.   *(Genesis 2:15)*

O God, the Creator of all things, you have imposed on us the obligation of work. May the example and prayer of blessed Joseph the Worker help us to accomplish the tasks you give us and to attain the reward you have promised. Through Christ our Lord. Amen.

FOR THOSE IN THE ARMED FORCES

Let us then pursue what makes for peace and for mutual upbuilding.   *(Romans 14:19)*

A Soldier's Prayer

Stay with us, Lord, for each of us has need of you. We are all in this together now, and need you more than ever. We want you to be a part of our team, O Lord. You know each of us as we are — our good points, our faults, our ups and downs. Help us to live, work, play and pray better together as real, mature men and women should.

O Lord, I pray for all the others whom you know need special graces from you right now; for those with whom I have difficulty getting along or those whom I always seem to rub the wrong way. Help me to see them more as you do, and let me not judge any one for what I dislike in them. Guide and direct all our shared thoughts, words, efforts and actions so that, through our contacts with one another, we may become better persons during this time we are in service here together.

Above all, let no one be less than he or she could be because of me. Yes, bless us all, O Lord. Amen.

FOR ALL SOLDIERS

O God, kindly watch over those exposed to the dangers of a soldier's life. Give them such strong faith that nothing may ever lead them to deny it or fear to practice it. Fortify them by your grace against the contagion of bad example, so that, preserved from vice and serving you faithfully, they may be ready to meet death if it should come.

Most Sacred Heart of Jesus, inspire them with sorrow for sin and grant them pardon. Mary, our Mother, be with them in battle, and should they be called upon to make the supreme sacrifice, obtain for them the grace to die in the love of your divine Son. St. Joseph, pray for them. Amen.

For Sailors and Marines

O God, almighty and most gracious, we acknowledge your dominion on earth and in the heavens, and the infinite love manifested in your relationship with us. As the Creator you have made the world and invited us to share in its development; as the Redeemer, you save the world and invite us to participate in its salvation. Give to those who ply the sea, our sailors and marines, the wisdom and courage to so live and sacrifice that, with justice maintained and true liberty safeguarded, all people everywhere may be possessed of that peace which you alone can give. As they travel the trackless seas with your stars for guidance, or plod their weary way along mountain or jungle trails, be with them, their constant support and their ultimate goal. May they know your continuous care as they give of themselves that others may know security and peace. Amen.

A Pilot's Prayer

Lord God, we are ever mindful of the responsibilities which are ours in the armed forces of our country. Help us to see and understand the wisdom of your laws, particularly of your commandment to love our neighbor as ourselves. This is a difficult task because of the confusion of our times. Yet with your help we can appreciate the depths of your love for all human beings. You have called all people to freedom and justice in the image and the spirit of your Son, Jesus Christ.

We beseech you, God, to strengthen and protect those of us who are engaged in dangerous missions of flight.

Inspire us and give us courage to be more fully human
so that your kingdom of peace, justice, and love may
be experienced by all peoples in this global village
which we call the world.

For the opportunity of serving you and our country,
we thank you and praise you in the name of your Son,
Jesus. Amen.

THE PRAYER OF ONE IN THE COUNTRY'S SERVICE

Give me clean hands,
  clean words,
    clean thoughts.
Help me to stand
  for the hard right
    against the easy wrong.
Save me from the habits that harm.

Teach me to work as hard
  and play as fair in your sight alone
    as if all the world could see.

Forgive me when I am unkind
  and help me to forgive
    those who are unkind to me.

Keep me ready to help others
  at some cost to myself.
Send me chances to do a little good
  every day,
And so grow more like you, O Lord,
  my brother and my Savior!

PRAYERS FOR THE SICK

SCRIPTURE READINGS FOR THE SICK

Are any among you sick? They should call for the elders of the church and have them pray over them, anointing them with oil in the name of the Lord. The prayer of faith will save the sick, and the Lord will raise them up; and anyone who has committed sins will be forgiven. *(James 5:14-15)*

IN THE NAME OF JESUS, WALK

One day Peter and John were going up to the temple at the hour of prayer, at three o'clock in the afternoon. And a man lame from birth was being carried in. People would lay him daily at the gate of the temple called the Beautiful Gate so that he could ask for alms from those entering the temple. When he saw Peter and John about to go into the temple, he asked them for alms. Peter looked intently at him, as did John, and said, "Look at us." And he fixed his attention on them, expecting to receive something from them. But Peter said, "I have no silver or gold, but what I have I give you; in the name of Jesus Christ of Nazareth, stand up and walk." And he took him by the right hand and raised him up; and immediately his feet and ankles were made strong. Jumping up, he stood and began to walk, and he entered the temple with them, walking and leaping and praising God. All the people saw him walking and praising God, and they recognized him as the one who used to sit and ask for alms at the Beautiful Gate of the temple; and they were filled with wonder and amazement at what had happened to him. *(Acts 3:1-10)*

While he clung to Peter and John, all the people ran together to them in the portico called Solomon's Portico, utterly astonished. When Peter saw it, he addressed the people, "You Israelites, why do you wonder at this, or why do you stare at us, as though by our own power or piety we had made him walk? The God of Abraham, the God of Isaac, and the God of Jacob, the God of our ancestors has glorified his servant Jesus, whom you handed over and rejected in the presence of Pilate, though he had decided to release him. But you rejected the Holy and Righteous One and asked to have a murderer given to you, and you killed the Author of life, whom God raised from the dead. To this we are witnesses. And by faith in his name, his name itself has made this man strong, whom you see and know; and the faith that is through Jesus has given him this perfect health in the presence of all of you.   *(Acts 3:11-16)*

HE TOOK OUR SICKNESSES AWAY

Now when he came into Capharnaum a centurion came up to him, appealing to him and saying, "Lord, my servant is lying paralyzed at home, terribly tormented." And he said to him, **"I'll come heal him."** And in response the centurion said, "Lord, I'm not worthy to have you come under my roof, but just say the word and my servant will be healed. For I, too, am a man under authority and have soldiers under me, and I say to this one, 'Go!' and he goes, and to another, 'Come!' and he comes, and to my slave, 'Do this!' and he does it." Now when Jesus heard this he was amazed and said to those who were following, **"Amen, I say to you, nowhere have I found such faith in Israel! I tell you, many will come from east and west and will recline at table with Abraham and Isaac and Jacob in the Kingdom of Heaven, but the sons of the kingdom will be thrown out into the outer darkness;**

> **There, there will be wailing
> and gnashing of teeth!"**

And Jesus said to the centurion, **"Go your way! Let it be done for you as you have believed."** And his servant was cured at that very moment.

(Matthew 8:5-13)

Jesus Cures Many

And after leaving there Jesus went along the sea of Galilee, and he ascended the mountain and sat down there. Large crowds came to him who had with them lame, blind, crippled, dumb people, and many others, and they put them down at his feet and he cured them, so that the crowd marvelled when they saw the dumb speaking, cripples sound, and the lame walking and the blind seeing, and they glorified the God of Israel.

(Matthew 15:29-31)

You Did It to Me

> **"But when the Son of Man comes in his glory,
> and all his angels with him,
> He'll sit on the throne of his glory,
> and all the nations will be gathered
> together before him,**

And he'll separate them from each other,
  like a shepherd separates the sheep
    from the goats,
And he'll set the sheep at his right hand
    and the goats at his left hand.

"Then the king will say to those
      at his right hand,
    'Come, you blessed of my Father,
  Receive the kingdom prepared for you
    from the foundation of the world,

For I was hungry and you gave me to eat,
  I was thirsty and you gave me to drink,
  I was a stranger and you took me in,
    naked and you clothed me,
  I was sick and you cared for me,
    I was in prison and you came to me.'

"Then the righteous will answer him by saying,
  'Lord, when did we see you hungry and feed
      you,
    or thirsty and give you to drink?
And when did we see you a stranger
    and take you in,
    or naked and clothe you?
And when did we see you sick,
    or in prison and come to you?'

"And in answer the king will say to them,
    'Amen, I say to you,
  Insofar as you did it for one of these least
    of my brothers,
    you did it for me.' "

(Matthew 25:31-40)

And he said to them, **"Go into the whole world and proclaim the good news to all creation. Whoever believes and is baptized will be saved, but whoever doesn't believe will be condemned. These signs will follow with those who believe -- they'll drive out demons in my name, they'll speak in new tongues, they'll pick up snakes in their hands, and if they drink poison it won't harm them; they'll lay their hands on the sick and they'll be well."**

Then the Lord, after speaking to them, was raised up to heaven and took his seat at the right hand of God. But they went out to proclaim [the good news] everywhere, the Lord working with them and confirming the word through the signs following upon it.
(Mark 16:15-20)

ASK, AND IT WILL BE GIVEN YOU

And he said to them, **"If any of you had a friend and went to him at midnight and said to him, 'Friend, lend me three loaves -- my friend has arrived on a journey to me and I haven't a thing to set before him,' would he answer from inside, 'Don't bother me! The door's already locked and my children are with me in the bed; I can't get up and give you anything.' I tell you, even if he doesn't get up and give him something because he's his friend, he'll get up and give him whatever he needs out of a sense of shame. So to you I say,**

Ask! and it shall be given to you;
  Seek! and you shall find;
    Knock! and it shall be opened to you.

For everyone who asks, receives;
Whoever seeks will find;
  And to those who knock it shall be opened.

But is there a father among you who,
  if his son asks for a fish,
    instead of a fish will hand him a snake?
Or if he asks for an egg,
  will hand him a scorpion?
So if you who are evil know how
  to give good gifts to your children,
How much more will the Father from heaven
  give the Holy Spirit to those who ask him!"
(Luke 11:5-13)

SINS SHALL BE FORGIVEN

So when it was evening on that first day of the week, and the doors had been locked where the disciples were for fear of the Jews, Jesus came and stood in their midst and said to them, **"Peace be with you!"** And after saying this he showed them his hands and side. The disciples rejoiced to see the Lord. So he said to them again, **"Peace be with you! As the Father has sent me, I, too, send you."** And after saying this he breathed on them and said, **"Receive the Holy Spirit!**

> **Whoever's sins you forgive,**
>   **they've already been forgiven;**
> **Whoever's you retain,**
>   **they've already been retained."**
(John 20:19-23)

FOR HEALTH

Heal me, O LORD, and I shall be healed;
  save me, and I shall be saved;
  for you are my praise.   *(Jeremiah 17:14)*

FOR A SICK PERSON

Almighty God, giver of health and healing, grant to
your servant a palpable sense of your presence and
perfect trust in you. In suffering may he (she) cast his
(her) care on you, so that, enfolded in your love and
power, he (she) may receive health and salvation
according to your gracious will. Through Christ our
Lord. Amen.

FOR ONE'S SELF WHEN ILL

Dear Lord, you are the great physician. I turn to you in
my sickness and ask you to help me.

Put your hand upon me as you did for people long ago
and let health and wholeness come into me from you.
I put myself under your care and affirm my faith that
even now your marvelous healing grace is making me
well and strong again.

I know that I ask more than I deserve but you never
measure our benefits on that basis. You just love us
back into health. Do that for me, I earnestly ask, and
I will try to serve you more faithfully. This I promise
through Christ our Lord. Amen.

FOR PEACE OF MIND

Let us therefore approach the throne of grace with boldness, so that we may receive mercy and find grace to help in time of need.   *(Hebrews 4:16)*

A Prayer of Hope

Our heavenly Father, as the sun brightens the earth and gives it warmth and life, it reminds us of your love. For it is in you that we live and move and have our being. As you have been with us many times during difficulties in the past, so continue to bless us with your help now.

Look graciously upon your servant and bless all that is done to care for this child of yours who is sick. Guide with wisdom and skill the physicians and all others who minister to those who are ill. Lend your healing forces so that health and strength may be restored. We will always be thankful for your generous and loving care. Amen.

Prayer When Worried

Dear Lord, I'm worried and full of fear. Anxiety and apprehension fill my mind. Could it be that my love for you is weak and imperfect and as a result I am plagued by worry?

I have tried to reassure myself that there is nothing to worry about. But such reassurances do not seem to help. I know that I should just rest myself confidently on your loving care and guidance. But I have been too upset even to pray.

Touch me, dear Lord, with your peace, and help my disturbed spirit to know that you are God and that I need fear no evil.

BEFORE AN OPERATION

Loving Father, I entrust myself to your care this day; guide with wisdom and skill the minds and hands of those who heal in your name. Grant that with every cause of illness removed, I may be restored to sound health, and learn to live in more perfect harmony with you and with my neighbor. Through Jesus Christ. Amen.

AFTER AN OPERATION

Blessed Savior, I thank you that this operation is safely past, and now I rest in your abiding presence, relaxing every tension, releasing every care and anxiety, receiving more and more of your healing life into every part of my being.

In moments of pain I turn to you for strength; in times of loneliness I feel your loving nearness. Grant then that your life and love and joy may flow through me for the healing of others in your name. Amen.

FOR A SICK CHILD

And he took a child and stood it in the middle of them, and he put his arms around it and said to them,

> **"Whoever receives one such child in my name receives me;**
> **And whoever receives me,**
> **receives not me but the One who sent me."**
> *(Mark 9:36-37)*

O Jesus, you welcomed children to come to you that you might lay your hand on them to bless them. We beg you to extend your hand in blessing upon this child to ease its pain and to heal it of all infirmity. By your mercy may this little one be restored to health of body and mind, so that with a grateful heart it may love and serve you. Through Christ our Lord. Amen.

St. Gerard, who like the Savior loved children tenderly, and by your prayers freed many from disease and even from death, graciously look down upon the distressed parents who plead with you for their child's health, if such be the will of God. Present their promise to God to raise the child as a good Christian and to guard it by word and example against the fatal disease of sin. This favor we implore you, O sainted brother, through the tender love with which Jesus and Mary blessed your own innocent childhood. Amen.

FOR THE APPREHENSIVE AND THE DEPRESSED

Therefore, since we are justified by faith, we have peace with God through our Lord Jesus Christ, through whom we have obtained access to this grace in which we stand; and we boast in our hope of sharing the glory of God. And not only that, but we also boast in our sufferings, knowing that suffering produces endurance, and endurance produces character, and character produces hope, and hope does not disappoint us, because God's love has been poured into our hearts through the Holy Spirit that has been given to us. *(Romans 5:1-5)*

FOR THE APPREHENSIVE PATIENT

Christ said to his loved ones: "I am with you, fear not, be not anxious." May I, then, be confident that in the trials and crosses of my life that you, O Lord, will be my constant companion. Whenever I cannot stand, you will carry me lovingly in your arms.

May I have no fear of what may happen tomorrow. For the same eternal Father who cares for me today will take care of me tomorrow and every day of my life. You, O Lord, will either shield me from suffering or give me strength to bear it patiently. May I be at peace, then, and put aside all useless thoughts, anxieties, and worries. Amen.

FOR THE DEPRESSED PATIENT

Praise to you, O Christ, and honor and glory! As your passion drew nearer, you began to know weariness and depression. Thus you took upon yourself the weakness of our human nature that you might strengthen and console those who are fearful of serious illness. I beg you to free me from all discouragement and anxiety. Grant that all I endure may be to your glory and for the pardon of my sins. Deliver me from faintheartedness and all unreasonable fears, and fix my heart firmly and unwaveringly on you. Amen.

FOR A PERSON WHO IS UNCONSCIOUS

As we have shared much in the suffering of Christ, so through Christ do we share abundantly in his consolation. If we are being afflicted, it is for your consolation and salvation; if we are being consoled, it is for your consolation, which you experience when you patiently endure the same sufferings that we are also suffering. Our hope for you is unshaken; for we know that as you share in our sufferings, so also you share in our consolation.   *(2 Corinthians 1:5-7)*

Remind us, O Lord, that all things work together for the good of those who love you. Comfort your child who is presently unconscious and quickly restore your servant to health. Assure him (her), when consciousness returns, that you will enable him (her) to wait for your healing with patience, for your peace with hope, and for your house of many mansions with faith. Amen.

FOR ONE'S DOCTORS

Honor physicians for their services, for the Lord created
       them;
    their gift of healing comes from the Most High,
        and they are rewarded by the king.
The skill of physicians makes them distinguished,
    and in the presence of the great they are admired.
                                        (Sirach 38:1-3)

Thank you, O Lord, for my doctors. Give them insight that they may understand and diagnose. Steady their hands by your strong hand. Look over their shoulder, O Lord, and endow them with power to heal in your name. Through Jesus Christ our Lord. Amen.

TO OUR LADY, FOR HELP IN TIME OF ILLNESS

    Better off poor, healthy, and fit
      than rich and afflicted in body.
    Health and fitness are better than any gold,
      and a robust body than countless riches.

There is no wealth better than health of body,
and no gladness above joy of heart.

(Sirach 30:14-16)

Virgin, most holy, Mother of the Word Incarnate and refuge of sinners, I fly to your motherly affection with lively faith, and I beg of you the grace always to do the will of God.

Into your most holy hands I commit the keeping of my heart, asking you for health of soul and body in the certain hope that you, most loving Mother, will hear my prayer.

Into your tender mercy, I commend my soul and body this day, every day of my life, and at the hour of my death.

To you I entrust all my hopes and consolations, all my trials and miseries, my life and the end of my life, so that all my actions may be ordered and disposed according to your will and that of your divine Son. Amen.

FOR COMMUNION OF THE SICK

For I received from the Lord what I also handed on to you, that the Lord Jesus on the night when he was betrayed took a loaf of bread, and when he had given thanks, he broke it and said, **"This is my body that is for you. Do this in remembrance of me."** In the same way he took the cup also, after supper, saying, **"This cup is the new covenant in my blood. Do this, as often as you drink it, in remembrance of me."** For as often as you eat this bread and drink the cup, you proclaim the Lord's death until he comes.

(1 Corinthians 11:23-26)

Lord Jesus Christ, you assumed a human body out of love for us. You loved us even unto death and washed us in your blood. In the sacrament of your love you remain with us and give us yourself as food.

Have mercy on us, and be with us! Lord Jesus Christ, you are the Bread of Life. Whoever comes to you will not hunger. Whoever believes in you will not thirst. You came from heaven, not to do your own will, but the will of him who sent you. The bread that you give us is your flesh for the life of the world. Those who eat your flesh and drink your blood shall have everlasting life, and you will awaken them on the last day. For your flesh is truly food and your blood is really drink. Those who eat your flesh and drink your blood remain in you and you remain in them. As the heavenly Father lives in you and you in him, so too will those who eat your flesh live through you. Amen.

PRAYERS FOR THE DYING AND THE DECEASED

A SPIRITUAL TESTAMENT

**"For this is the will of my Father,
that everyone who sees the Son and believes
in him should have eternal life.
Such a one will I raise up on the last day."**

(John 6:40)

I love God with my whole heart and soul. I desire to love the Lord, my God, with the love with which all the saints, and especially our Blessed Mother, have loved him.

Because I love God, I am heartily sorry for all the sins that I have ever committed against my Lord and against my neighbor.

For the love of God, I also forgive with all my heart all those who have ever offended me or have shown themselves to be my enemies.

I ask pardon of all whom I have ever offended in word or deed. Amen.

FOR PERSEVERANCE AND MERCY

"So stay awake! because you don't know what day your Lord is coming. Be sure of this, though. If the householder had known at what watch the thief was coming he would have stayed awake and wouldn't have let his house be broken into. Therefore, you be ready too! because the Son of Man is coming at an hour you don't expect."

(Matthew 24:42-44)

For Perseverance

O Lord, you submitted yourself to death to be an example and comfort to your servants at their own hour of death. Be near the dying at this moment, we beg you. Quiet their fears, strengthen their faith, and confirm their hopes. Obeying your call, may they meet you readily and cheerfully. Lord Jesus, strengthen them with your grace, help them to accept your holy will with constancy and perseverance, and to give themselves completely to you. Amen.

For Mercy

My God! I turn to you, I call upon you, I trust in you, to your infinite goodness I entrust my entire life. I have sinned exceedingly. Enter not, O Lord, into judgment with me, your servant. I surrender to you and confess my guilt. Of myself, I cannot make satisfaction for my countless sins. I have not the wherewithal with which to pay you, and my debt is infinite. But your Son has shed his blood for me, and your mercy is greater than all my iniquity. Amen.

Offering at the Hour of Death

O Jesus! As I think of your dying moments, I beseech you to receive mine. Not knowing whether I shall have command of my senses as I leave this world, I offer you, even now, my last agony and all the anguish of my passing. Since you are my Savior, I give back my soul into your hands. Grant that the last beat of my heart may be an act of perfect love toward you. Amen.

Your will, not mine, be done. Amen.

I believe in you, I hope in you. I love you. I adore you. Blessed Trinity, one God, have mercy on me now and save me at the hour of my death. Amen.

FOR A HOLY DEATH

Almighty and merciful God, you have bestowed on us both the remedies of health and the gifts of life everlasting. Look mercifully upon us, your servants, and refresh the souls which you have made that, at the hour of our death, we may be found worthy to be presented without stain of sin to you, our Maker, by the hands of your holy angels. Amen.

O my Lord and Savior,
   support me in my last hour
in the strong arms of your sacraments
   and by the power of
your consolations.

Let the absolving words be said over me,
   and the holy oil sign and seal me;
And let your own body be my food,
   and your blood my sprinkling,
and let my Mother, Mary, breathe on me
   and my angel whisper peace to me.

And my glorious saints and my own
   patrons smile upon me that,
in them all and through them all,
   I may receive the gift of perseverance,
and die as I desire to live—
   in your Church,
   in your service,
   and in your love. Amen.

(Cardinal Newman)

LITANY FOR THE DYING

Jesus answered them,

> **"I told you and you don't believe.**
> **The works I do in the name of my Father—**
> **these bear witness to me,**
> **But you don't believe because you're not**
> **from among my sheep."** *(John 11:25-26)*

In reparation for all my sins, may God help me to bear with patience the sufferings and pains of my sickness and weakness.

Lord, have mercy on us.
Christ, have mercy on us.
Lord, have mercy on us. Christ, hear us.
Christ, graciously hear us.

God the Father of heaven, *have mercy on us.*
God the Son, Redeemer of the world, *have mercy on us.*
God the Holy Spirit, *have mercy on us.*
Holy Trinity, one God, *have mercy on us.*

Holy Mary, *pray for him (her).*
All you holy angels and archangels, *pray for him (her).*
Holy Abel, *pray for him (her).*
All you choirs of the just, *pray for him (her).*
Holy Abraham, *pray for him (her).*
St. John the Baptist, *pray for him (her).*
St. Joseph, *pray for him (her).*
All you holy patriarchs and prophets, *pray for him (her).*
St. Peter, *pray for him (her).*
St. Paul, *pray for him (her).*
St. Andrew, *pray for him (her).*
St. John, *pray for him (her).*

All you holy apostles and evangelists, *pray for him (her)*.
All you holy disciples of the Lord, *pray for him (her)*.
All you holy innocents, *pray for him (her)*.
St. Stephen, *pray for him (her)*.
St. Lawrence, *pray for him (her)*.
All you holy martyrs, *pray for him (her)*.
St. Sylvester, *pray for him (her)*.
St. Gregory, *pray for him (her)*.
St. Augustine, *pray for him (her)*.
All you holy bishops and confessors, *pray for him (her)*.
St. Benedict, *pray for him (her)*.
St. Francis, *pray for him (her)*.
St. Camillus, *pray for him (her)*.
St. John of God, *pray for him (her)*.
All you holy monks and hermits, *pray for him (her)*.
St. Mary Magdalen, *pray for him (her)*.
St. Lucy, *pray for him (her)*.
All you holy virgins and widows, *pray for him (her)*.
All you holy saints of God, *make intercession for him (her)*.

Be merciful, *spare him (her), O Lord!*
Be merciful, *deliver him (her), O Lord!*

From your wrath, *O Lord, deliver him (her)*.
From the peril of death, *O Lord, deliver him (her)*.
From a painful death, *O Lord, deliver him (her)*.
From the pains of hell, *O Lord, deliver him (her)*.
From all evil, *O Lord, deliver him (her)*.
From the power of the devil, *O Lord, deliver him (her)*.
Through you birth, *O Lord, deliver him (her)*.
Through your cross and passion, *O Lord, deliver him (her)*.
Through your death and burial, *O Lord, deliver him (her)*.

— 66 —

Through your glorious resurrection, *O Lord, deliver him (her)*.

Through your admirable Ascension, *O Lord, deliver him (her)*.

Through the grace of the Holy Spirit, the Comforter, *O Lord, deliver him (her)*.

In the day of judgment, we sinners *beseech you, hear us*.
That you spare him (her), *we beseech you, hear us*.

Lord, have mercy.
Christ, have mercy.
Lord, have mercy.

O God most merciful, O God most loving, O God who, according to the multitude of your mercies, forgives the sins of the penitent and graciously remits all the guilt of their past offenses, look favorably upon your servant, and grant him (her) full remission of all his (her) sins.

Renew within him (her), O most loving Father, whatever has been corrupted through human frailty or violated through the deceits of the devil. Make him (her) a true member of the Church, and let him (her) partake of the fruit of your redemption. Have pity on him (her) in his (her) tears, O Lord, and admit him (her), who has no hope but in you, to the joy of your reconciliation. Through Christ our Lord. Amen.

IN THE LAST AGONY AND AT THE MOMENT OF DEATH

We will not all die, but we will all be changed, in a moment, in the twinkling of an eye, at the last trumpet. For the trumpet will sound, and the dead will be raised imperishable, and we will be changed. For this perishable body must put on imperishability, and this mortal body must put on immortality. When this perishable body puts on imperishability, and this mortal body puts on immortality, then the saying that is written will be fulfilled:

> "Death has been swallowed up in victory."
> "Where, O death, is your victory?
> Where, O death, is your sting?"
>
> *(1 Corinthians 15:52-55)*

In the Last Agony

When death is imminent, then more than ever, the relatives and friends ought to pray earnestly on their knees around the sick person's bed. If the dying person is unable to speak, the name of Jesus should constantly be invoked, and such prayers as the following should be repeated.

Into your hands, O Lord, I commend my spirit. O Lord Jesus Christ, receive my spirit. Holy Mary, pray for me. O Mary, Mother of grace, Mother of mercy! Protect me from the enemy, and receive me at the hour of death. Amen.

St. Joseph, pray for me. St. Joseph, in company with the blessed Virgin, your spouse, obtain for me the divine mercy of Jesus. Amen.

Jesus, Mary, and Joseph! I give you my heart, my soul and my life.

Jesus, Mary, and Joseph! Assist me in my last agony.

Jesus, Mary, and Joseph! May I breathe forth my soul in peace with you. Amen.

Go forth from this world, O Christian soul, in the name of God the Father almighty who created you; in the name of Jesus Christ the Son of the living God, who suffered for you; in the name of the Holy Spirit, who has been poured forth upon you; in the name of the Holy Mother of God, the Virgin Mary; in the name of St. Joseph, her illustrious spouse. May peace by your dwelling today, and may your home be in heaven with your God. Through Christ our Lord. Amen.

I commend you to almighty God and I entrust you to him who created you, so that you may return to your Lord after you leave this mortal life. When by dying you have paid the debt to which everyone is subject, may you return to your Maker who formed you from the clay of the earth. Then when your soul goes forth from your body, may the holy Mother of God lovingly turn her eyes toward you and may the angels lead you into the heavenly paradise which God has prepared for you since the beginning of the world. Amen.

May Christ, who was crucified for your sake, free you from excruciating pain. May Christ, who died for you, free you from everlasting death. May Christ, the Son of the living God, set you in the loveliness of his paradise, and may he, the true shepherd, recognize you as one of his own. May he free you from all your sins, and assign you a place at his right hand in the company of his elect in heaven. May you see your Redeemer face-to-face, and standing in his presence forever, may you see with joyful eyes your Maker and Savior revealed in all his fullness. And so, having taken your place in the ranks of the blessed in heaven, may you enjoy the happiness of divine contemplation forever and ever. Amen.

Holy Mary, Mother of God! Pray for me now and at the hour of my death.

My guardian angel, my holy patron saints! Do not abandon me at the hour of my death.

St. Joseph! Obtain for me the grace of dying the death of a saint.

Jesus, Mary, and Joseph, bless us now and in the agony of death.

Grant, we beseech you, O Lord, that in the hour of our death we may be refreshed by your holy sacraments and freed from all guilt. May we thus deserve to be received with joy into the arms of your mercy. Through Christ our Lord. Amen.

Lord Jesus! Infuse into our hearts the spirit of your love, that in the hour of our death we may overcome the enemy and attain the heavenly crown.

I commend you to almighty God, whose creature you are, and commit you to his mercy, that when you have paid the debt of humanity by death, you may return to your Maker who formed you out of the earth.

May the bright company of angels meet you.
May the court of the apostles receive you.
May the triumphant army of glorious martyrs
    conduct you.
May the choir of blessed virgins go before you.
May a happy rest be your portion in the company of the patriarchs.
May St. Joseph, the patron of the dying, inspire you with great confidence.

May Mary, the holy Mother of God, turn her eyes in mercy upon you, and may Jesus Christ give you a place among those who are to be in his presence for ever. Amen.

AFTER THE DEATH OF A LOVED ONE

We seem to give them back to you, O God, who first gave them to us. Yet as you did not lose them in giving, so do we not lose them by their return. Not as the world gives, do you give. What you give you do not take away, for what is yours is ours also if we are yours. And life is eternal, and love is immortal, and death is only a horizon; and a horizon is nothing save the limit of our sight.

Lift us up, strong Son of God, that we may see further. Remove the scales from our eyes that we may see more clearly; draw us closer to you that we may know ourselves to be nearer to our loved ones who are with you. And while you prepare a place for us, prepare us also for that happy place, that where you are we may also be forever. Amen.

Come to his (her) aid, O saints of God; hasten to meet him (her), angels of the Lord. Take up his (her) soul, and present it in the sight of the Most High.

V. May you be received by Christ, who has called you; and may the angels bring you into the bosom of Abraham.

R. Taking up your soul, and presenting it in the sight of the Most High.

AFTER A SUDDEN DEATH

He said, "Jesus, remember me when you come into your kingdom!" And he said to him, **"Amen, I say to you, this day you'll be with me in paradise."** (Luke 23:42-43)

O almighty God, you give to each of us the breath of life and sustain it until life's final moment. We humbly commend to your loving care your servant whom you have called suddenly to yourself. We beg you to be a merciful Savior to him (her), cleansing him (her) from every sin by the blood of Jesus crucified so that he (she) may enjoy life everlasting. This we ask through the merits of Jesus Christ your only Son, our Lord. Amen.

O Lord Jesus Christ, you are the resurrection and the life. You have promised that those who believe in you, even if they die, will have life everlasting. May this sacred promise comfort us in our sadness that we may take solace in the hope of a life after death. Help us to realize that those who die believing in you will live forever. O Savior of the world, reassure us in our belief that death is not an end of life, but rather a change by which we enter a life of perfect joy in Christ Jesus. Amen.

AFTER THE DEATH OF A CHILD

But we do not want you to be uninformed, brothers and sisters, about those who have died, so that you may not grieve as others do who have no hope. For since we believe that Jesus died and rose again, even so, through Jesus, God will bring with him those who have died. For this we declare to you by the word of the Lord, that we who are alive, who are left until the coming of the Lord, will by no means precede those who have died. For the Lord himself, with a cry of command, with the archangel's call, and with the sound of God's trumpet, will descend from heaven, and the dead in Christ will rise first. Then we who are alive, who are left, will be caught up in the clouds together with them to meet the Lord in the air; and so we will be with the Lord forever. Therefore, encourage one another with these words.

(1 Thessalonians 4:13-18)

O Jesus, you said, "Let the little children come to me and do not hinder them, for to such belongs the kingdom of heaven." Then you took them into your arms and blessed them, laying your hands upon them.

We beg you, O Lord, to protect this precious one in your arms. Bless, preserve, and keep this little child and grant it complete contentment and security in your love.

Strengthen, O Lord, the parents who are stricken with grief because of the loss of their little one. Help them to realize, as they question why this should happen to their child, that your ways are not our own. O Jesus, let the hope of being reunited with their child at the glorious resurrection be a source of consolation to them. Amen.

FOR DECEASED BISHOPS AND PRIESTS

I have fought the good fight, I have finished the race, I have kept the faith. From now on there is reserved for me the crown of righteousness, which the Lord, the righteous judge, will give me on that day, and not only to me but also to all who have longed for his appearing.   *(2 Timothy 4:7-8)*

O God, who raised your servants to the dignity of the apostolic priesthood, grant, we ask you, that they may be joined in fellowship with your apostles forevermore. Through Christ our Lord. Amen.

FOR ALL THE FAITHFUL DEPARTED

But if he was looking to the splendid reward that is laid up for those who fall asleep in godliness, it was a holy and pious thought. Therefore he made atonement for the dead, so that they might be delivered from their sin.

(2 Maccabees 12:43-45)

O Lord, the Creator and Redeemer of all the faithful, grant to the souls of your servants departed the remission of all their sins that, by the humble supplications of your Church, they may obtain the pardon which they have always desired of your mercy. Amen.

Eternal rest grant unto them, O Lord, and let perpetual light shine upon them. May they rest in peace. Amen.

PRAYERS FOR PERSONAL FULFILLMENT

BASIC DAILY PRAYERS

"When you pray,
don't be like the hypocrites -
They love to pray standing in the synagogues
and on the corners of wide streets,
so people will notice them.
Amen, I say to you,
they have their full reward!

But when you pray,
go into your storeroom and, when you've
closed the door,
Pray to your Father who is hidden,
and your Father who sees what's hidden
will reward you."

"When you're praying,
don't babble on like the Gentiles -
They think they'll be heard
because of their wordiness.
But don't be like them,
for your Father knows what you need
before you ask Him."

(Matthew 6:5-8)

MY DAILY PRAYER

I believe in one God. I believe that God rewards the good and punishes the wicked.

I believe that in God there are three divine Persons — the Father, the Son, and the Holy Spirit.

I believe that God the Son became man, without ceasing to be God. I believe that he is my Lord and Savior, the Redeemer of the human race, that he died on the cross for the salvation of all, that he died also for me. I believe in God's authority, in everything that he has taught and revealed.

O my God, give me strong faith. O my God, help me to believe with lively faith.

O my God, who is all-good and all-merciful, I sincerely hope to be saved. Help me to do all that is necessary for my salvation.

I have committed many sins in my life but now I turn away from them and hate them. I am sorry, truly sorry, for all of them, because I have offended you, my God, who are all-good, all-perfect, all-holy, all-merciful and kind.

I love you, my God, with all my heart. Please forgive me for having offended you.

I promise, O God, that with your help I will never offend you again.

My God, have mercy on me!

ACT OF FAITH

**"Amen, amen, I say to you,
Whoever believes has eternal life."**

(John 6:47)

O my God, I firmly believe that you are one God in three divine Persons, Father, Son, and Holy Spirit. I believe that your divine Son became man, died for our sins, and that he will come to judge the living and the dead. I believe these and all the truths which the holy Catholic Church teaches, because you have revealed them, who can neither deceive nor be deceived.

So then, brothers and sisters, stand firm and hold fast to the traditions that you were taught by us, either by word of mouth or by our letter. Now may our Lord Jesus Christ himself and God our Father, who loved us and through grace gave us eternal comfort and good hope, comfort your hearts and strengthen them in every good work and word.

(2 Thessalonians 2:15-17)

O my God, relying on your almighty power and infinite mercy and promises, I hope to obtain pardon of my sins, the help of your grace, and life everlasting through the merits of Jesus Christ, my Lord and Redeemer.

ACT OF LOVE

Beloved, let us love one another, because love is from God; everyone who loves is born of God and knows God. Whoever does not love does not know God, for God is love. *(1 John 4:7-8)*

O my God, I love you above all things, with my whole heart and soul, because you are all-good and worthy of all love. I love my neighbor as myself for the love of you. I forgive all who have injured me, and ask pardon of all whom I have injured. Amen.

ACT OF CONTRITION

Rend your hearts and not your clothing.
　Return to the LORD, your God,
for he is gracious and merciful,
　slow to anger, and abounding in steadfast love,
　and relents from punishing.　*(Joel 2:13)*

O my God, I am heartily sorry for having offended you.
I detest all my sins, because I dread the loss of heaven
and the pains of hell, but most of all because they
offend you, my God, who are all-good and deserving of
all my love. I firmly resolve, with the help of your
grace, to confess my sins, to do penance, and to amend
my life. Amen.

FOR THE DAY

Pray in the Spirit at all times in every prayer and
supplication. To that end keep alert and always
persevere in supplication for all the saints.
(Ephesians 6:18)

Christ as a light, illumine and guide me!
Christ as a shield, o'ershadow and cover me!
Christ be under me! Christ be over me!
Christ be before me, behind me, and about me!
Christ be this day within and without me!
Christ, lowly and meek; Christ, all-powerful, be
In the hearts of all to whom I speak,
On the lips of all who speak to me.
(The Breastplate of St. Patrick)

Mend a quarrel.
  Search out a forgotten friend.
Dismiss suspicion and
  replace it with trust.
Write a loving letter.
  Share some treasure
Give a soft answer.
  Encourage a youth.
Manifest your loyalty
  in word or in deed.

Keep a promise.
  Find the time.
Forgo a grudge.
  Forgive an enemy.
Listen.
  Apologize if you were wrong.
Try to understand.
  Flout envy.
Examine your demands on others.
  Think first of someone else.
Appreciate, be kind, be gentle.
  Laugh a little more.

Deserve confidence.
  Take up arms against malice.
Decry complacency.
  Express your gratitude.
Worship your God.
  Gladden the heart of a child.
Take pleasure in the beauty
  and the wonder of the earth.
Speak your love.

Speak it again.
Speak it still again.
Speak it still once again.

FOR INNER PEACE AND SERENITY

**"Peace I leave with you,
my peace I give to you;
Not as the world gives
do I give to you.
Let not your hearts be troubled
nor afraid."** *(John 14:27)*

God, Grant me the

Serenity to accept the things I cannot change;
Courage to change the things I can; and
Wisdom to know the difference.
Living one day at a time
Enjoying one moment at a time
Accepting the hardships as the pathway to peace
Taking, as He did, his sinful world as it is,
not as I would have it
Trusting that He will make all things right
if I surrender to his will
That I may be reasonably happy in this life
and supremely happy with him forever in the next.
Amen.

FOR CHRISTLIKE VIRTUE

If I speak in the tongues of mortals and of angels, but do not
have love, I am a noisy gong or a clanging cymbal. And if I
have prophetic powers, and understand all mysteries and all
knowledge, and if I have all faith, so as to remove mountains,

but do not have love, I am nothing. If I give away all my possessions, and if I hand over my body so that I may boast, but do not have love, I gain nothing.

Love is patient; love is kind; love is not envious or boastful or arrogant or rude. It does not insist on its own way; it is not irritable or resentful; it does not rejoice in wrongdoing, but rejoices in the truth. It bears all things, believes all things, hopes all things, endures all things.

(1 Corinthians 13:1-8)

For Charity

O God, you make all things work together unto good for those who love you; give to our hearts an abiding love for you, that the desires we conceive by your inspiration may ever remain unchanged in spite of every temptation. Through Christ our Lord. Amen.

For Humility

For if those who are nothing think they are something, they deceive themselves. *(Galatians 6:3)*

O God, you resist the proud and bestow grace on the humble. Grant us the virtue of true humility of which your only-begotten Son showed himself an example to the faithful, that we may never provoke you to anger by our pride, but rather receive through humility the gifts of your grace. Amen.

For Generosity

If you have many possessions, make your gift from them in proportion; if few, do not be afraid to give according to the little you have. Thus you will be laying up a good treasure for yourself against the day of necessity. *(Tobit 4:8-9)*

Jesus, teach me to be generous,

To serve you as you deserve to be served —

to give and not count the cost;

to fight and not heed the wounds;

to toil and not seek rest;

to labor and not ask any reward

except that of knowing that I do your holy will.

My God, you are all powerful;

Give me the grace of heroic holiness.

FOR THE OFFERING OF SELF

Receive, O Lord, all my liberty. Take my memory, my understanding, and my whole will. Whatever I have, whatever I possess, you have given to me. I restore it all to you. I yield it to be ruled directly by your will. Give me only your love and your grace, and I am rich enough; nor do I ask for more.

LEARNING OF CHRIST

Teach me, my Lord, to be sweet and gentle in all the events of life — in disappointments, in the thoughtlessness of others, in the insincerity of those I trusted, in the unfaithfulness of those on whom I relied. Let me put myself aside to think of the happiness of others, and to hide my little pains and heartaches, so that I may be the only one to suffer from them.

Teach me to profit by the suffering that comes across my path. Let me so use it that it may mellow me, not harden or embitter me; that it may make me patient, not irritable; that it may make me broad in my forgiveness, not narrow, haughty, and overbearing.

May no one be less good for having come within my influence - no one less pure, less true, less kind, less noble for having been a fellow traveler in our journey toward eternal life.

As I go my rounds from one distraction to another, let me whisper from time to time, a word of love to you. May my life be lived in the supernatural, full of power for good, and strong in its purpose of sanctity.

Lord Jesus, I unite myself to your perpetual, unceasing, universal sacrifice. I offer myself to you every day of my life and every moment of every day, according to your most holy and adorable will. You have been the victim of my salvation; I wish to be the victim of your love. Accept my desire, take my offering, graciously hear my prayer. Let me live for love of you; let me die for love of you; let my last heartbeat be an act of perfect love. Amen.

To the Holy Spirit

And because you are children, God has sent the Spirit of his Son into our hearts, crying, "Abba! Father!"
(Galatians 4:6)

I am going to reveal to you the secret of sanctity and happiness. Every day for five minutes control your imagination, close your eyes to the things of sense and your ears to the noise of the world, in order to enter into yourself. There, in the sanctuary of your baptized Spirit, say to him:

"O Holy Spirit, beloved of my soul, I adore you. Enlighten me, guide me, console me. Tell me what I must do; give me your orders. I promise to subject myself to all that you desire of me and to accept all that you permit to happen to me. Let me only know your will."

If you do this, your life will flow along happily, serenely, and full of consolation even in the midst of trials. Grace will be proportioned to the trial, giving you strength to carry it, and you will arrive at the gate of paradise laden with merit. This submission to the Holy Spirit is the secret of sanctity.

(Cardinal Mercier)

Come, Holy Spirit,
> Replace the tension within us
> > with a holy relaxation.
> Replace the turbulence within us
> > with a sacred calm.
> Replace the anxiety within us
> > with a quiet confidence.
> Replace the fear within us
> > with a strong faith.
> Replace the bitterness within us
> > with the sweetness of grace.
> Replace the darkness within us
> > with a gentle light.
> Replace the coldness within us
> > with a loving warmth.
> Replace the night within us
> > with your day.
> Replace the winter within us
> > with your spring.
> Straighten our crookedness,
> > Fill our emptiness,

Dull the edge of our pride,
   Sharpen the edge of our humility,
Light the fires of our love,
   Quench the flames of our lust.
Let us see ourselves as you see us.
   That we may see you as you have promised.
And be fortunate according to your word:
   "Blessed are the pure of heart,
      for they shall see God."

PRAYERS FOR SPECIAL NEEDS

"Amen, amen, I say to you, whatever you ask the Father for in my name He'll give you. Up till now you've asked for nothing in my name; ask and you'll receive, so your joy may be complete." *(John 16:23-24)*

FOR CONTINENCE

To the clean all things are clean. *(1 Titus 1:15)*

Enkindle, O Lord, our being and our hearts with the fire of the Holy Spirit, that we may serve you with a chaste body and please you with a pure heart.

FOR PATIENCE

With all humility and gentleness, with patience, bear with one another in love, making every effort to maintain the unity of the Spirit in the bond of peace.
(Ephesians 4:2-3)

O God, who by the patience of your only begotten Son crushed the pride of the enemy of old, grant us, we beg you, the grace devoutly to keep in mind all he endured for love of us and thus, by following his example, to bear our troubles with equanimity. Amen.

> Although I've asked God every day,
> These many anxious years,
> And yet the blessing has not come,
> I still believe he hears!
>
> I know that he does answer prayer
> Sometimes unseen to man,
> Then I shall trust and wait till I
> Can see God's deeper plan.
>
> Perhaps the things for which I prayed,
> Were not the best for me,
> But till I know, I'll importune,
> And trust God patiently.

FOR PERSEVERANCE

Rejoice in hope, be patient in suffering, persevere in prayer. *(Romans 12:12)*

We adore you, O Holy Trinity. We reverence you. We thank you with humblest sentiments of gratitude for having revealed to us this most glorious and incomprehensible mystery.

Grant that by persevering in this faith until death, we may see and glorify in heaven what we believe here below on earth -- one God in three divine Persons: the Father, the Son, and the Holy Spirit. Amen.

FOR CONFIDENCE IN GOD

By contrast, the fruit of the Spirit is love, joy, peace, patience, kindness, generosity, faithfulness, gentleness, and self-control. There is no law against such things. *(Galatians 5:22)*

Why, O LORD, do you stand far off?
    Why do you hide yourself in times of trouble?
In arrogance the wicked
        persecute the poor —
    let them be caught in the schemes they have
            devised.

For the wicked boast of the desires of their heart
    those greedy for gain curse and renounce the
            LORD.
In the pride of their countenance the wicked say,
        "God will not seek it out";
    all their thoughts are, "There is no God."

Their ways prosper at all times;
    your judgments are on high,
        out of their sight;
    as for their foes, they scoff at them.
They think in their heart, "We shall not be moved;
    throughout all generations we shall not meet
            adversity."

Their mouths are filled with
        cursing and deceit and oppression;
    under their tongues are mischief and iniquity.
They sit in ambush in the villages;
    in hiding places they murder the innocent.

Their eyes stealthily watch for the helpless;
    they lurk in secret like a lion in its covert;
they lurk that they may seize the poor;
    they seize the poor and drag them off in their net.

They stoop, they crouch,
    and the helpless fall by their might.

They think in their heart, "God has forgotten,
　　he has hidden his face, he will never see it."

Rise up, O LORD; O God, lift up your hand;
　　do not forget the oppressed.
Why do the wicked renounce God,
　　and say in their hearts, "You will not call us to
　　　　account"?
But you do see! Indeed you note trouble and grief,
　　that you may take it into your hands;
　　the helpless commit themselves to you;
　　　　you have been the helper of the orphan.

Break the arm of the wicked and evildoers;
　　seek out their wickedness until you find none.
The LORD is king forever and ever;
　　the nations shall perish from his land.

O LORD, you will hear the desire of the meek;
　　you will strengthen their heart, you will incline your
　　　　ear
to do justice for the orphan and the oppressed,
　　so that those from earth may strike terror no more.
　　　　　　　　　　　　　　　　(Psalm 10:1-18)

Let nothing disturb you,
　　Nothing affright you;
All things are passing
　　God never changes.
Patient endurance
　　Attains to all things;
Who God possesses
　　In nothing is wanting.
Alone God suffices.

(St. Teresa's Bookmark)

PART 2

SPECIAL DEVOTIONS

FIAT VOLUNTAS TUA

MORNING PRAYER

*To pray with one another is to pray with Christ, for
"wherever two or three are gathered in my name, there
am I in the midst of them." To pray a liturgical type
morning prayer is to echo the prayer of Christ in his
Church. This morning prayer is suitable for private use,
and it may be used also by those who pray together.*

In the name of the Father, and of the Son, and of the Holy
Spirit. Amen.

God, come to my assistance. Lord, make haste to help me.

Glory be to the Father, and to the Son, and to the Holy Spirit;
as it was in the beginning, is now, and ever shall be, world
without end. Amen.

HYMN

Glory in the heights to God;
  on earth, peace;
  to men, favor.
We praise you,
  bless you,
  worship you,
  laud you.
We give you thanks
  for your great glory,
O Lord, King of heaven
God the Father all-powerful,
Lord, the only Son,
  Jesus Christ,
and you, Holy Spirit.

O Lord God,
  God's Lamb,
  the Father's Son,
You take the world's sins away:
  have mercy on us.
You take the world's sins away:
  accept our prayer.
You sit at the Father's right hand:
  have mercy on us.

For you alone are holy,
  you alone are Lord,
O Jesus Christ,
  for God the Father's glory.
                    Amen.

PSALM 31

In you, O LORD, I seek refuge;
    do not let me ever be put to shame;
    in your righteousness deliver me.
Incline your ear to me;
    rescue me speedily.
Be a rock of refuge for me,
    a strong fortress to save me.

You are indeed my rock and my fortress;
    for your name's sake lead me and guide me,
take me out of the net that is hidden for me,
    for you are my refuge.
Into your hand I commit my spirit;
    you have redeemed me,
        O LORD, faithful God.

You hate those who pay regard to worthless idols,
  but I trust in the LORD.
I will exult and rejoice in your steadfast love,
  because you have seen my affliction;
  you have taken heed of my adversities,
and have not delivered me
  into the hand of the enemy;
  you have set my feet in a broad place.

Be gracious to me, O LORD, for I am in distress;
  my eye wastes away from grief,
  my soul and body also.
For my life is spent with sorrow,
  and my years with sighing;
my strength fails because of my misery,
  and my bones waste away.

I am the scorn of all my adversaries,
  a horror to my neighbors,
an object of dread to my acquaintances;
  those who see me in the street flee from me.
I have passed out of mind like one who is dead;
  I have become like a broken vessel,
For I hear the whispering of many —
  terror all around! —
as they scheme together against me,
  as they plot to take my life.

But I trust in you, O LORD;
  I say, "You are my God."
My times are in your hand;
  deliver me from the hand
  of my enemies and persecutors.
Let your face shine upon your servant;

save me in your steadfast love.
Do not let me be put to shame, O LORD,
   for I call on you;
let the wicked be put to shame;
   let them go dumbfounded to Sheol.
Let the lying lips be stilled
   that speak insolently against the righteous
   with pride and contempt.

O how abundant is your goodness
   that you have laid up for those who fear you,
   and accomplished for those who take refuge in you,
   in the sight of everyone!
In the shelter of your presence
   you hide them from human plots;
you hold them safe under your shelter
   from contentious tongues.

Blessed by the LORD,
   for he has wondrously shown his steadfast love to me
   when I was beset as a city under siege.
I had said in my alarm,
   "I am driven far from your sight."
But you heard my supplications
   when I cried out to you for help.

Love the LORD, all you his saints.
The LORD preserves the faithful,
   but abundantly repays the one who acts haughtily.
Be strong, and let your heart take courage,
   all you who wait for the LORD.   *(Psalm 31)*

Glory be to the Father and to the Son, and to the Holy Spirit;
as it was in the beginning, is now, and ever shall be, world
without end. Amen.

SONG OF DAVID

"Blessed are you, O LORD,
    the God of our ancestor Israel,
    forever and ever.
Yours, O LORD, are the greatness, the power,
    the glory, the victory, and the majesty;
for all that is in the heavens and on the earth is yours;
    yours is the kingdom, O LORD,
    and you are exalted as head above all.
Riches and honor come from you,
    and you rule over all.
In your hand are power and might;
    and it is in your hand to make great
    and to give strength to all.
And now, our God, we give thanks to you
    and praise your glorious name.

(1 Chronicles 29:10-13)

Glory be to the Father and to the Son, and to the Holy Spirit;
as it was in the beginning, is now, and ever shall be, world
without end. Amen.

PSALM 29

Ascribe to the LORD, O heavenly beings,
    ascribe to the LORD glory and strength,
Ascribe to the LORD the glory of his name;
    worship the LORD in holy splendor.

The voice of the LORD is over the waters;
    the God of glory thunders,
    the LORD, over mighty waters.
The voice of the LORD is powerful;
    the voice of the LORD is full of majesty.

The voice of the LORD breaks the cedars;
   the LORD breaks the cedars of Lebanon.
He makes Lebanon skip like a calf,
   and Sirion like a young wild ox.

The voice of the LORD flashes forth flames of fire.
The voice of the LORD shakes the wilderness;
   the LORD shakes the wilderness of Kadesh.

The voice of the LORD causes the oaks to whirl,
   and strips the forest bare;
   and in his temple all say, "Glory!"

The LORD sits enthroned over the flood;
   the LORD sits enthroned as king forever.
May the LORD give strength to his people!
   May the LORD bless his people with peace!

(Psalm 29)

Glory be to the Father and to the Son, and to the Holy Spirit;
as it was in the beginning, is now, and ever shall be, world
without end. Amen.

WORD OF GOD

Besides this, you know what time it is, how it is now the
moment for you to wake from sleep. For salvation is nearer
to us now than when we became believers; the night is far
gone, the day is near. Let us then lay aside the works of
darkness and put on the armor of light; let us live honorably
as in the day not in reveling and drunkenness, not in debauch-
ery and licentiousness, not in quarreling and jealousy. Instead, put on the Lord Jesus Christ, and make no provision
for the flesh, to gratify its desires.   *(Romans 13:11-14)*

THE BENEDICTUS

"Blessed be the Lord God of Israel —
    He has visited and set His people free,
And He has raised up a horn of salvation for us
    in the house of His servant David,
Just as He promised through the mouths of His
       holy prophets from of old:
       to save us from our enemies and from the hand
       of all who hate us;
To show mercy to our fathers
    and be mindful of His holy covenant,
Of the oath he swore to our father Abraham,
    to grant us, saved from the hand
       of enemies,
That we might worship Him without fear,
    in holiness and righteousness,
    in His presence all our days.
And you, child, will be called a prophet
       of the Most High,
    for you will go before the Lord to prepare
       his ways,
To give knowledge of salvation to His people
    by forgiving their sins,
Through the tender mercy of our God,
    whereby the Shining Light from on high
       will visit us,
To give light to those in darkness and
       in the shadow of death,
    to guide our feet into the way of peace."

(Luke 1:68-79)

Glory be to the Father and to the Son, and to the Holy Spirit; as it was in the beginning, is now, and ever shall be, world without end. Amen.

PRAYERS

With firm confidence that we can hope in your promise, "Ask and you shall receive, seek and you shall find," we address our needs to you, O Father:

That we are your creatures, and in you live and move and have our being, *let us always be grateful to you, O Lord.*

That we are your children, born to you in baptism, and destined to be most loving children who share your happiness, *let us always be grateful to you, O Lord.*

That we are engaged in a lifelong opportunity to serve you and those to whom we are committed by responsibility and vocation, *let us always be grateful to you, O Lord.*

That we have only one commandment — to love one another — and are surrounded only by brothers and sisters, *let us always be grateful to you, O Lord.*

THE LORD'S PRAYER

Our Father, who art in heaven, hallowed be thy name; thy kingdom come; thy will be done on earth as it is in heaven. Give us this day our daily bread; and forgive us our trespasses as we forgive those who trespass against us; and lead us not into temptation, but deliver us from evil. Amen.

May you support us all the day long, till the shades lengthen, and the evening comes, and the busy world is hushed, and the fever of life is over, and our work is done. Then in your mercy may you give us a safe lodging, and a holy rest, and peace at the last. Amen.

Before today's round of experience, labor, and joy, we direct our thoughts and motives to you, O Lord. Be with us in the beginning and in the completion of everything we do. Let all that we do be done in the name of your Son, our Lord Jesus Christ, who lives and reigns with you, in the unity of the Holy Spirit, one God, forever and ever. Amen.

EVENING PRAYER

*The joys and sorrows of another day's living can inspire
varied themes in prayer — a reassured faith, a painful
pleading, occasionally a need for forgiveness, but always
praise and thanksgiving. This evening prayer is modelled
on the official prayer of the Church.*

In the name of the Father, and of the Son, and of the Holy
Spirit. Amen.

God, come to my assistance. Lord, make haste to help me.

Glory be to the Father, and to the Son, and to the Holy Spirit;
as it was in the beginning, is now, and ever shall be, world
without end. Amen.

HYMN

Inspiring light, O holy glory
of the undying, heavenly Father,
the holy, the blessed,
Jesus Christ:
the sun has set now,
seeing the lamp that lights the evening,
we praise the Father and the Son
and God the Holy Spirit.

PSALM 27

The LORD is my light and my salvation;
  whom shall I fear?
The LORD is the stronghold of my life;
  of whom should I be afraid?

When evildoers assail me
  to devour my flesh —
my adversaries and foes —
  they shall stumble and fall.

Though an army encamp against me,
  my heart shall not fear;
though war rise up against me,
  yet I will be confident.

One thing I asked of the LORD,
  that will I seek after:
to live in the house of the LORD
  all the days of my life,
to behold the beauty of the LORD,
  and to inquire in his temple.

For he will hide me in his shelter
  in the day of trouble;
he will conceal me under the cover of his tent;
  he will set me high on a rock.

Now my head is lifted up
  above my enemies all around me,
and I will offer in his tent
  sacrifices with shouts of joy;
I will sing and make melody to the LORD.

Hear, O LORD, when I cry aloud,
  be gracious to me and answer me!
"Come," my heart says, "seek his face!"
  Your face, LORD, do I seek.
  Do not hide your face from me.

Do not turn your servant away in anger,
  you who have been my help.

do not cast me off, do not forsake me,
  O God of my salvation!
If my father and mother forsake me,
  the LORD will take me up.

Teach me your way, O LORD,
  and lead me on a level path
  because of my enemies.
Do not give me up to the will of my adversaries,
  for false witness have risen against me,
  and are breathing out violence.

I believe that I shall see the goodness of the LORD
  in the land of the living.
Wait for the LORD;
  be strong, and let your heart take courage;
  wait for the LORD.   *(Psalm 27:1-14)*

Glory be to the Father, and to the Son, and to the Holy Spirit; as it was in the beginning, is now, and ever shall be, world without end. Amen.

EPHESIANS 1:3-14

Blessed be the God and Father of our Lord Jesus Christ, who has blessed us in Christ with every spiritual blessing in the heavenly places, just as he chose us in Christ before the foundation of the world to be holy and blameless before him in love. He destined us for adoption as his children through Jesus Christ, according to the good pleasure of his will, to the praise of his glorious grace that he freely bestowed on us in the Beloved.

In him we have redemption through his blood, the forgiveness of our trespasses, according to the riches of his grace that he lavished on us. With all wisdom and insight he has made known to us the mystery of his will, according to his good pleasure that he set forth in Christ, as a plan for the fullness of time, to gather up all things in him, things in heaven and things on earth.

In Christ we have also obtained an inheritance, having been destined according to the purpose of him who accomplishes all things according to his counsel and will, so that we, who were the first to set our hope on Christ, might live for the praise of his glory. In him you also, when you had heard the word of truth, the gospel of your salvation, and had believed in him, were marked with the seal of the promised Holy Spirit; this is the pledge of our inheritance toward redemption as God's own people, to the praise of his glory.

Glory be to the Father, and to the Son, and to the Holy Spirit; as it was in the beginning, is now, and ever shall be, world without end. Amen.

WORD OF GOD

If I speak in the tongues of mortals and of angels, but do not have love, I am a noisy gong or a clanging cymbal. And if I have prophetic powers, and understand all mysteries and all knowledge, and if I have all faith, so as to remove mountains, but do not have love, I am nothing. If I give away all my possessions, and if I hand over my body so that I may boast, but do not have love, I gain nothing.

Love is patient; love is kind; love is not envious or boastful or arrogant or rude. It does not insist on its own way; it is not irritable or resentful; it does not rejoice in wrongdoing, but rejoices in the truth. It bears all things, believes all things, hopes all things, endures all things. *(1 Corinthians 13:1-8)*

THE MAGNIFICAT

"My soul gives praise to the Lord,
  and my spirit rejoices in God my Savior;
Because He had regard for the lowliness
    of His handmaid,
  behold, henceforth all generations shall
    call me blessed,
For the Mighty One has done great things for me,
  and holy is His name,
And His mercy is from generation to generation
  toward those who fear Him.
He has shown might with His arm,
  scattered the arrogant in the conceit
    of their heart,
He has pulled down the mighty from their thrones,
  and exalted the lowly,
The hungry he has filled with good things,
  and has sent the rich away empty.
He has come to the aid of His servant, Israel,
  mindful of His mercy,
Just as He promised our fathers,
  Abraham and his descendants forever."

(Luke 1:46-55)

Glory be to the Father, and to the Son, and to the Holy Spirit; as it was in the beginning, is now, and ever shall be, world without end. Amen.

PRAYERS

Confident that God will look with mercy on prayers which are offered with a humble and sincere heart, we pray:

That those who do not yet respond in faith to Christ will soon be joined to the Church in faith and baptism,

we fervently pray.

That those who have the courage to be peacemakers may succeed in laying the groundwork of peace and be rewarded as Christ promised, *we fervently pray.*

That those who are worn by the tension which comes with change and growth may remember the parables of the kingdom of God, and be open to God's action,

we fervently pray.

That we may know the responsibilities of a vocation, and respond with determination to the opportunity to live it,

we fervently pray.

That all who have died in Christ may experience the glory and the fulfillment of resurrection unto eternal life,

we fervently pray.

THE LORD'S PRAYER

Our Father, who art in heaven, hallowed be thy name; thy kingdom come; thy will be done on earth as it is in heaven. Give us this day our daily bread; and forgive us our trespasses as we forgive those who trespass against us; and lead us not into temptation, but deliver us from evil. Amen.

Be close to those who are faithful to you, O Lord, as they come to the end of another day; it resembles the end which someday will come to life. As we turn to you in humble and hopeful prayer, give us both contrition for our sins and the confidence that they have been forgiven. Lead us through a lifetime to things eternal, but be open to our needs at every stage of the journey. Through Christ our Lord. Amen.

PRAYERS BEFORE RETIRING

Who will separate us from the love of Christ? Will hardship, or distress, or persecution, or famine, or nakedness, or peril, or sword? As it is written,

> "For your sake we are being
> killed all day long;
> we are accounted as sheep
> to be slaughtered."

No, in all these things we are more than conquerors through him who loved us. For I am convinced that neither death, nor life, nor angels, nor rulers, nor things present, nor things to come, nor powers, nor height, nor depth, nor anything else in all creation, will be able to separate us from the love of God in Christ Jesus our Lord.   *(Romans 8:35-39)*

> Into your hands, O Lord, I commend my spirit.
> Into your hands, O Lord, I commend my spirit.
> You have redeemed us, O Lord, God of truth,
> Into your hands, I commend my spirit.

Glory be to the Father, and to the Son, and to the Holy Spirit.

> Into your hands, O Lord, I commend my spirit.

Protect us, Lord, while we are awake and safeguard us while we sleep, that we may keep watch with Christ and rest in peace.

> Now, Master, you can dismiss your servant in peace;
>   you have fulfilled your word.
> For my eyes have witnessed your saving deed
>   displayed for all the peoples to see:
> A revealing light to the Gentiles,
>   the glory of your people Israel.   *(Luke 2:29-32)*

Glory be to the Father, and to the Son, and to the Holy Spirit; as it was in the beginning, is now, and ever shall be, world without end. Amen.

Protect us, Lord, while we are awake, and safeguard us while we sleep, that we may keep watch with Christ and rest in peace.

Visit this house, O Lord, we beg you, and banish from it all the deadly power of the enemy. May your holy angels dwell herein to keep us in peace, and may your blessings be upon us always. We ask this through Christ, our Lord. Amen.

May the all-powerful and merciful Lord, Father, Son, and Holy Spirit, bless us and keep us. Amen.

May the divine assistance remain always with us. Amen.

PREPARATION FOR MASS

I bring to Mass today:

    — my hopes and my needs, my trials, and my fears;

    — my gratitude for all that I have received from my
Father's hand up to the present moment;

        — my desire to remain close to my Father and come
even closer to him during this day.

I come to the altar today:

        — to give thanks for the daily mystery of my redemp-
tion and salvation;

        — to seek the strength and perseverance that I find so
lacking in myself;

        — to seal again the covenant with God, my Father, in
and through Christ Jesus my Lord.

PREPARATION FOR HOLY COMMUNION

PSALM 84

How lovely is your dwelling place,
O LORD of hosts!
My soul longs, indeed it faints,
for the courts of the LORD;
my heart and my flesh sing for joy
to the living God.

Even the sparrow finds a home,
and the swallow a nest for herself,
where she may lay her young,
at your altars, O LORD of hosts,
my King and my God.
Happy are those who live in your house,
ever singing your praise.

Happy are those whose strength is in you,
in whose heart are the highways to Zion.
As they go through the valley of Baca
they make it a place of springs;
the early rain also covers it with pools.
They go from strength to strength;
the God of gods will be seen in Zion.

O LORD God of hosts, hear my prayer;
give ear, O God of Jacob!
Behold our shield, O God;
 look on the face of your anointed.
For a day in your courts is better
than a thousand elsewhere.
I would rather be a doorkeeper
in the house of my God
than live in the tents of wickedness.

For the LORD God is a sun and shield;
he bestows favor and honor.
No good thing does the LORD withhold
from those who walk uprightly.
O LORD of hosts, happy is everyone
            who trusts in you.   *(Psalm 84:1-12)*

DECLARATION OF INTENTION

Eternal Father, I unite myself with the intentions and affections of our Lady of Sorrows on Calvary, and I offer to you the sacrifice that your beloved Son Jesus made of himself upon the cross, and now renews upon this holy altar:

To adore you and give you the honor that is due to you, confessing your supreme dominion over all things, and the absolute dependence of everything upon you.

To thank you for the countless benefits that I have received.

To appease your justice, aroused against us by so many sins, and to make satisfaction for them.

To implore grace for myself, for *N.*, for all the afflicted and sorrowing, for poor sinners, for all the world, and for the holy souls in purgatory. Amen.

PRAYERS TO THE HOLY SPIRIT

O God, all hearts are open to you, and every wish and secret is known. Cleanse our thoughts by the inpouring of the Holy Spirit and grant us the grace to love you perfectly and praise you worthily.

May the holy Comforter, who proceeds from you, O Lord, enlighten our minds and teach us all truth, as your Son has promised.

O Lord, let the power of the Holy Spirit be with us, gently cleansing our hearts and guarding us against danger.

O God, you have instructed the hearts of the faithful by the light of the Holy Spirit. Grant that through the same Holy Spirit we may always be truly wise and rejoice in his consolation. Amen.

PRAYER OF ST. JOHN CHRYSOSTOM

I believe, Lord, and confess that you are truly Christ the Son of the living God, who came on earth to save sinners of whom I am chief, and I believe that this is your most pure body, and this your most precious blood.

I therefore pray you, have mercy upon me and forgive me my sins, in word and in deed..., voluntarily and knowingly committed; and vouchsafe unto me to partake without condemnation of your most pure mysteries, to the remission of sins and to life everlasting. Amen.

PRAYER OF ST. SIMEON

Behold, I approach the divine communion; my Creator, consume me not in the partaking of it, for you are a consuming fire to the unworthy. Purify me now from every stain.

Of your mysterious supper today, O Son of God, accept me as a partaker.

Into the brilliant company of your saints how shall I, unworthy and sinful, enter? If I dare to enter into the bridal chamber, my garment will put me to shame, for it is not a wedding one, and I shall be bound hand and foot and cast out by your angels. Purify, Lord, my soul, and save me in your loving kindness.

Master, lover of all, Lord Jesus Christ, my God, grant that I may not partake of these your holy mysteries to my condemnation because of my unworthiness, but to the purification and sanctification of my soul and body, and as a pledge of your everlasting life and kingdom.

For it is good for me to cleave unto my God, placing in the Lord the hope of my salvation.

THANKSGIVING AFTER MASS

Te Deum

You are God; we praise you;
You are the Lord; we acclaim you;
You are the eternal Father:
All creation worships you.

To you all angels, all the powers of heaven,
Cherubim and Seraphim, sing in endless praise:
    Holy, holy holy, Lord God of power and might,
    heaven and earth are full of your glory.

The glorious company of apostles praises you.
The noble fellowship of prophets praises you.
The white-robed army of martyrs praises you.

Throughout the world the holy Church acclaims you:
    Father of majesty unbounded,
    your true and only Son, worthy of all worship,
    and the Holy Spirit, advocate and guide.

You, Christ, are the king of glory,
    the eternal Son of the Father.
When you became man to set us free
    you did not spurn the Virgin's womb.
You overcame the sting of death,
    and opened the kingdom of heaven to all believers.
You are seated at God's right hand in glory.
    We believe that you will come and be our judge.
Come, then, Lord, and help your people,
    bought with the price of your own blood,
    and bring us with your saints
    to glory everlasting.

V. Save your people, Lord, and bless your inheritance.
R. Govern and uphold them now and forever.
V. Day by day we bless you.
R. We praise your name for ever.
V. Keep us today, Lord, from all sin.
R. Have mercy on us, Lord, have mercy.
V. Lord, show us your mercy and love;
R. for we put our trust in you.
V. In you, O Lord, is our hope,
R. and we shall never hope in vain.

PSALM 150

Praise the LORD!
Praise God in his sanctuary;
praise him in his mighty firmament!
Praise him for his mighty deeds;
praise him according to his surpassing greatness!

Praise him with trumpet sound;
praise him with lute and harp!
Praise him with tambourine and dance;
praise him with strings and pipe!
Praise him with clanging cymbals;
praise him with loud clashing cymbals!
Let everything that breathes
praise the LORD!
Praise the LORD!   *(Psalm 150:1-6)*

Prayer Before a Crucifix

Look down upon me, O good and gentle Jesus, while
before your face I humbly kneel and with the most fervent
desire of my soul, I pray and beseech you to fix deep in

my heart lively sentiments of faith, hope, and charity, true contrition for my sins and a firm purpose of amendment, while with deep affection and grief of soul I reflect upon and ponder over your five most precious wounds, having before my eyes the words which David spoke of you in prophecy: "They have pierced my hands and my feet; they have numbered all my bones."

PRAYER OF ST. THOMAS AQUINAS

I thank you, O Lord, holy Father, everlasting God, who through no merit of mine, but only out of your great mercy, have fed me, a sinner, your unworthy servant, with the precious body and blood of your Son, our Lord Jesus Christ; and I pray that this Holy Communion may not be for my judgment and condemnation, but for my pardon and salvation. Let it be for me an armor of faith and a shield of good purpose, a riddance of all vices, and a rooting out of all evil desires; an increase of love and patience, of humility and obedience, and of all virtues; a firm defense against the wiles of all my enemies, visible and invisible; a perfect quieting of all my impulses, carnal and spiritual; a cleaving unto you, the one true God; and a blessed consummation of my end when you call. And I pray that you would bring me, a sinner, to that ineffable feast where you, with your Son and the Holy Spirit, are to your holy ones true light, fullness of blessedness, everlasting joy, and perfect happiness. Through Christ our Lord. Amen.

Anima Christi

Soul of Christ, sanctify me.
Body of Christ, save me.
Blood of Christ, inebriate me.
Water from the side of Christ, wash me.
Passion of Christ, strengthen me.
O good Jesus, hear me.
Within your wounds hide me.
Permit me never to be separated from you.
From the malicious enemy defend me.
At the hour of my death call me
and bid me come to you
that, with your saints, I may praise you
forever and ever. Amen.

POINTS OF REFERENCE FOR
THE EXAMINATION OF CONSCIENCE

THE TEN COMMANDMENTS

1. I am the Lord thy God, who brought you out of the land of Egypt, and out of the house of bondage. You shall not have strange gods before me.
2. You shall not take the name of the Lord your God in vain.
3. Remember to keep holy the Sabbath day.
4. Honor your father and your mother.
5. You shall not kill.
6. You shall not commit adultery.
7. You shall not steal.
8. You shall not bear false witness against your neighbor.
9. You shall not covet your neighbor's wife.
10. You shall not covet your neighbor's goods.

THE PRECEPTS OF THE CHURCH

1. To hear Mass on Sundays and holydays of obligation.
2. To fast and abstain on the days appointed.
3. To confess at least once a year all grave sins.
4. To receive Holy Communion during the Easter season.
5. To contribute to the support of the Church.
6. To observe the laws of the Church concerning marriage.

THE CORPORAL WORKS OF MERCY

1. To feed the hungry.
2. To give drink to the thirsty.
3. To clothe the naked.
4. To visit those who are in prison.
5. To give shelter to the homeless.
6. To visit the sick.
7. To bury the dead.

THE SPIRITUAL WORKS OF MERCY

1. To admonish sinners.
2. To instruct the ignorant.
3. To counsel the doubtful.
4. To comfort the sorrowful.
5. To bear wrongs patiently.
6. To forgive all injuries.
7. To pray for the living and the dead.

THE BEATITUDES

Blessed are the poor in spirit,
  for theirs is the Kingdom of Heaven.
Blessed are those who are mourning,
  for they shall be comforted.

Blessed are the meek,
  for they shall inherit the earth.
Blessed are those who hunger and thirst
    for righteousness,
  for they shall have their fill.

Blessed are the merciful,
   for they shall receive mercy.
Blessed are the pure of heart,
   for they shall see God.

Blessed are the peacemakers,
   for they shall be called sons of God.
Blessed are those persecuted for the sake
     of righteousness,
   for theirs is the Kingdom of Heaven.

Blessed are you when they insult you and persecute and speak every evil thing against you for my sake; rejoice and be glad, because your reward will be great in the heavens — they persecuted the prophets before you in the same way.

(Matthew 5:3-12)

THE ROSARY

FIRST JOYFUL MYSTERY

THE ANNUNCIATION

Now in the sixth month the angel Gabriel was sent from God
to a city of Galilee named Nazareth, to a virgin who was
betrothed to a man of the house of David named Joseph, and
the virgin's name was Mary. And when he came into her
presence he said, "Hail, full of grace, the Lord is with you!"
Now she was perplexed by this saying and wondered what
sort of greeting this could be. And the angel said to her,

"Fear not, Mary —
    you have found grace before the Lord.
And, behold, you will conceive in your womb
      and will bear a son,
    and you shall name him Jesus.
He'll be great and will be called
      Son of the Most High,
    and the Lord God will give him the throne
      of his father, David,
And he'll reign over the house of Jacob forever,
    and his kingdom will have no end."

(Luke 1:26-32)

Reflections

— the wonder of receiving an invitation from God;
— the startling extent of the divine invitation to Mary;
— Mary's prayerfulness was a preparation to do God's
    will;

— Mary was as free as we are in making decisions;
— the simplicity, directness, and integrity of Mary's question;
— her willingness to be the servant of the Lord at whatever personal cost.

For Myself

— to try each day to wonder enough at God's goodness; to pray to find his will; to use my freedom to do his wishes; to give "enough" to him.

SECOND JOYFUL MYSTERY

The Visitation

Now in those days Mary set out and went with solicitude into the hill country to a city of Judah, and she came into the house of Zechariah and greeted Elizabeth. And it happened that when Elizabeth heard Mary's greeting the baby leapt in her womb, and Elizabeth was filled with the Holy Spirit and exclaimed with a loud cry, "Blessed are you among women, and blessed is the fruit of your womb! And how is it that the mother of my Lord should come to *me*? For, behold, when the sound of your greeting came into my ears, the baby in my womb leapt with a great joy. Blessed is she who believed that there would be a fulfillment of what was spoken to her by the Lord." *(Luke 1:39-45)*

Reflections

— Mary's concern for her cousin expressed in swift action;

— the thoughtfulness evidenced in Mary's visit to her
  cousin;
— the love shown in unassuming service;
— Mary praises God for all that has been done to her.

For Myself

— to express concern for others in deeds as well as words,
  thoughtfully, quietly, and with gratitude to God for the
  opportunity to do so.

THIRD JOYFUL MYSTERY

THE NATIVITY

Now Joseph, too, went up from Galilee, from the city of
Nazareth, to Judea to the city of David, which is called
Bethlehem, because he was of the house and family of
David, to be registered with Mary, who was betrothed to
him, who was pregnant. Now it happened that while they
were there the days for her to give birth were fulfilled, and
she gave birth to her firstborn son, and she wrapped him in
swaddling clothes and laid him in a manger, because there
was no room for them in the inn.   *(Luke 2:4-7)*

Reflections

— the simplicity of the surroundings and sublimity of the
  persons;
— the mystery of "God-with-us";
— the holy family "crowded out" of the inn;
— the peace that permeates the birth of Jesus.

For Myself

— to show more concern for people than for things; not to
crowd God and his children out of my life; not to lose
the peace that comes with closeness to the Lord.

FOURTH JOYFUL MYSTERY

THE PRESENTATION OF THE CHILD JESUS IN THE TEMPLE

And when the days of their purification according to the
Torah of Moses had passed, they took him up to Jerusalem to
present him to the Lord — as it is written in the Torah of the
Lord, **every firstborn male shall be called holy to the Lord**
— and to offer a sacrifice according to what is said in the
Torah of the Lord, **a pair of turtle doves or two young
pigeons.** *(Luke 2:22-24)*

Reflections

— every child is God's gift to parents, who must bring the
child back to God;
— cheerful obedience to God's law is characteristic of the
Holy Family;
— the joy of Anna and Simeon who have waited so long
for a Savior;
— the ever-deepening trust of Joseph and Mary in their
heavenly Father.

For Myself

— to find cause for joy in all God's children; to see the
image of Jesus in every child and every grown-up; to
trust my heavenly Father and my human brothers and
sisters.

FIFTH JOYFUL MYSTERY

THE FINDING OF THE CHILD JESUS IN THE TEMPLE

And his parents used to go to Jerusalem every year for the festival of the Passover. And when he was about to turn twelve — when they had gone up to Jerusalem in accordance with the custom of the feast and when they had fulfilled the days, while they were returning — the child Jesus remained in Jerusalem, and his parents didn't know. But since they thought he was in the group of travellers they went a day's journey and then looked for him among their relatives and acquaintances, and when they didn't find him they returned to Jerusalem in search of him. And it happened that after three days they found him in the temple, seated in the midst of the teachers, both listening to them and asking them questions, and all those listening to him were amazed at his intelligence and his answers. *(Luke 2:41-47)*

Reflections

— the terrible sadness of losing Jesus even for a short time;
— the deep, human concern of Joseph and Mary;
— the interest of Jesus in deepening his human knowledge of heavenly things.

For Myself

— to "look for Jesus everywhere"; to relish opportunities to learn more about him and his Father, to listen with an open mind and heart to those who speak with the Spirit of God.

FIRST SORROWFUL MYSTERY

THE AGONY IN THE GARDEN

Then Jesus came with them to a place called Gethsemane, and he said to the disciples, **"Sit here while I go over there and pray."** And he took Peter and the two sons of Zebedee along and he began to be upset and troubled. Then he said to them, **"My soul is greatly distressed, to the point of death; stay here and stay awake with me."** And he went ahead a little and fell face down in prayer, and he said, **"My Father, if it's possible, let this cup pass away from me, yet not as I wish but as you do."** *(Matthew 26:36-39)*

Reflections

— suffering in mind and heart occurred prior to the physical suffering of Jesus;
— our Lord's desire for the human companionship of the three disciples;
— his natural, instinctive desire that the cup pass him by;
— his conscious, willed subjection to his Father's will, even in this.

For Myself

— to view the mystery of suffering with the eyes of faith;
— to seek to understand and accept the Father's mysterious will; to overcome the impulse to complain about and reject God's "strange ways."

SECOND SORROWFUL MYSTERY

THE SCOURGING OF JESUS

Now when Pilate saw that he was doing no good, but instead a riot was beginning, he took water and washed his hands in full view of the crowd and said, "I'm innocent of this man's blood! See to it yourselves!" And in answer the whole people said, "His blood be upon us, and upon our children!" Then he released Barabbas to them, but he had Jesus scourged and handed him over to be crucified. *(Matthew 27:24-26)*

Reflections

— Pilate's behavior shows the terrible effects of unconcern, the desire not to be involved;
— Pilate can actually say, "The responsibility is yours" as he sends an innocent man to suffer and die!
— the thoughts of Mary while witnessing all this.

For Myself

— to accept involvement with the innocent and oppressed that is essential to the Christian; to be concerned; to "grieve with those who grieve," not merely in word or in theory but in fact.

THIRD SORROWFUL MYSTERY

THE CROWNING OF JESUS WITH THORNS

Then the governor's soldiers took Jesus along to the praetorium and gathered the whole cohort around him. And they stripped him and put a scarlet robe on him, and after weaving a crown of thorns they put it on his head and a reed in his right hand, and they knelt before him and mocked him, saying, "Hail, King of the Jews!" After spitting on him they'd take the reed and beat him over the head. And when they had mocked him they stripped the robe off him and dressed him in his own clothes and led him off to be crucified. *(Matthew 27:27-31)*

Reflections

— the Son of God did not come to earth to share our crowns, but our crosses;
— in Jesus, God enters into our lives and we "make fun" of him;
— Jesus is "led away" by those he wishes to lead to eternal life.

For Myself

— to be sensitive to the ever-increasing role of Jesus in my life; to expect that every follower of Jesus will "be made fun of" by the world; to keep new crowns of thorns away from the brothers and sisters of the Lord.

FOURTH SORROWFUL MYSTERY

JESUS CARRIES THE CROSS

Now as they were going out they found a man named Simon of Cyrene; they forced this man to carry his cross.

(Matthew 27:32)

— Jesus carries the cross and falls under its weight; Mary walks the way of the cross with him; Simon helps; Veronica wipes his face; the women weep;
— the weight of the cross and the weight of sin; the destruction of human life that comes from sin; the destruction of divine life in ourselves that comes from sin.

For Myself

— to recognize my own vocation to "follow the blood-stained footprints" of my Lord; to find the true cross in my own life; to assist others to carry their crosses.

FIFTH SORROWFUL MYSTERY

THE CRUCIFIXION

And they brought him to the place called Golgotha, which, translated, is The Place of the Skull. And they tried to give him wine mixed with myrrh, but he didn't take it. And they crucified him,

> and his **clothes were divided up,**
> **casting lots for them** to see
> who would take what.

Now it was the third hour when they crucified him. And the inscription of the charge against him was written, "The King of the Jews." And they crucified two robbers with him, one on his right and one on his left. *(Mark 15:22-27)*

Reflections

— always the terrible physical cruelty; the nails, the thirst, the overwhelming pain;

— in addition, the depression and desolation, the feeling of abandonment;

— and always, the love and forgiveness extended even to the most cruel and the most uncaring.

For Myself

— to bear all sufferings for the sake of Jesus in a spirit of forgiveness; to fill up in myself "what is lacking in the sufferings of Christ" for his body which is the Church.

FIRST GLORIOUS MYSTERY

THE RESURRECTION

But in response the angel said to the women, "Don't be afraid — I know that you're seeking Jesus, who was crucified. He isn't here — he's risen, just like he said; come see the place where he lay. And go quickly to tell his disciples, 'He's risen from the dead and, behold, he's going ahead of you into Galilee; you'll see him there.' Behold, I've told you!"

(Matthew 28:5-7)

Reflections

— the resurrection is proof of our faith in Jesus and also a pledge of the resurrection from death of all who believe in him;

— his appearance — to Mary, to the devout women, to the disciples on the way to Emmaus, to the apostles and to Thomas —demonstrate the literal reality of the resurrection;

— the appearances of Jesus after the resurrection are characterized by the gift of peace.

For Myself

— to appreciate that it is only through faith in Jesus that I can hope that I "will not taste death forever"; to keep before me the glory of resurrection when I experience the terrors of the cross.

SECOND GLORIOUS MYSTERY

THE ASCENSION

When he had said this, as they were watching, he was lifted up, and a cloud took him out of their sight. While he was going and they were gazing up toward heaven, suddenly two men in white robes stood by them. They said, "Men of Galilee, why do you stand looking up toward heaven? This Jesus, who has been taken up from you into heaven, will come in the same way as you saw him go into heaven."

(Acts 1:9-11)

Reflections

— Jesus returns to heaven to sit at his Father's right hand as Lord and Savior, "always living to intercede for us";

— the work Jesus commenced on earth — "to bring to all people the Good News of salvation" — is now to be continued by all the members of his Church;

— he will come again in the same way, and the joy of his faithful ones will have no end.

For Myself

— to join myself consciously with the present grateful prayer of Christ our Priest; to prize the call to continue his work on earth; to live each day in the spirit of the prayer, "Come, Lord Jesus!"

THIRD GLORIOUS MYSTERY

THE DESCENT OF THE HOLY SPIRIT UPON THE APOSTLES

When the day of Pentecost had come, they were all together in one place. And suddenly from heaven there came a sound like the rush of a violent wind, and it filled the entire house where they were sitting. Divided tongues, as of fire, appeared among them, and a tongue rested on each of them. All of them were filled with the Holy Spirit and began to speak in other languages, as the Spirit gave them ability.

(Acts 2:1-4)

Reflections

— Jesus, who is "filled with the Holy Spirit," now sends the same Holy Spirit to his brothers;
— it is this Holy Spirit the Spirit of Jesus, that makes us truly children of God who can call him, "Father";

— the sharing of the Holy Spirit is the actual sharing of divine life.

For Myself

— to "recognize my dignity" as a sharer in the Holy Spirit; to strengthen my devotion to the Holy Spirit within me; to listen for the will of the Spirit every day in everything.

FOURTH GLORIOUS MYSTERY

THE ASSUMPTION OF THE BLESSED VIRGIN INTO HEAVEN

So it is with the resurrection of the dead. What is sown is perishable, what is raised is imperishable. It is sown in dishonor, it is raised in glory. It is sown in weakness, it is raised in power. It is sown a physical body, it is raised a spiritual body. If there is a physical body, there is also a spiritual body. *(1 Corinthians 15:42-44)*

Reflections

— Mary is in every way the closest associate of Jesus in the whole work of redemption;
— the full effect of redemption -- the conquest of death -- is shown to us in her assumption into heaven;
— the collaboration of Son and Mother on our behalf continues in heaven.

For Myself

— to see the realism of Mary's position in the work of her Son; to appreciate Mary as Mother of the Church; to seek the help of our Lady and her divine Son every moment "now and at the hour of death."

FIFTH GLORIOUS MYSTERY

And Mary said,
> "My soul gives praise to the Lord,
>   and my spirit rejoices in God my Savior;
> Because He had regard for the lowliness
>   of His handmaid,
>   behold, henceforth all generations shall
>   call me blessed,
> For the Mighty One has done great things for me,
>   and holy is His name."   *(Luke 1:46-49)*

Reflections

— the outward simplicity and lowliness of Mary's life contrasted with the actuality of her position in God's plan;

— Mary, the Queen of mercy, of compassion, of constant care for all her spiritual children;

— God in crowning our works crowns his own goodness, "Holy is his name!"

For Myself

— to seek an eternal crown even at the cost of present lowliness; to seek a crown of wisdom, justice, and peace; to acknowledge always that it is God himself who begins in us and brings to completion every good work.

THE STATIONS OF THE CROSS

FIRST STATION

JESUS IS CONDEMNED TO DEATH

Then he released Barabbas to them, but he had Jesus scourged and handed him over to be crucified.   (Matthew 27:26)

V. We adore you, O Christ, and we praise you.

R. Because by your holy cross you have redeemed the world.

Reflections

— Why? Hostility due to jealousy, envy, the loss of comfort and security because of his "blasphemy" in telling the truth.
— Why? His Father's mysterious will that Jesus win all people by being completely open, even to our cruelty and injustice.

For Myself

— to know that there is no path for me but that which Jesus trod; no plan but his Father's will; no entrance to glory but through a cross.

SECOND STATION

JESUS BEARS HIS CROSS

Then he handed him over to them to be crucified. So they took Jesus in charge. And carrying the cross himself he went out to what was called "The Place of the Skull," in Hebrew, "Golgotha." *(John 19:16-17)*

V. We adore you, O Christ, and we praise you.
R. Because by your holy cross you have redeemed the world.

Reflections

— "Shall I crucify your king?" "We have no king but Caesar"; total rejection by his people under the guise of righteousness;
— crucifixion of a criminal with other criminals. But what was the terrible crime? "I am come that they may have life and have it more abundantly."
— would it be different now? Is it different now?

For Myself

— to know that it always remains possible to reject Jesus and his brothers and sisters under the cover of self-righteous virtue; to help others bear their crosses as we would like to have helped Jesus.

THIRD STATION

Jesus Falls the First Time

He began to teach them that the Son of Man had to suffer greatly and be rejected by the elders and the chief priests and the scribes and be put to death and rise after three days; and he spoke, saying this openly. So Peter took him aside and began to remonstrate with him.   *(Mark 8:31-32)*

V. We adore you, O Christ, and we praise you.
R. Because by your holy cross you have redeemed the world.

Reflections

— the evident physical weakness of our Lord would seem enough to rouse the sympathy of even a hardened soul;
— the weakness of Jesus is always something of a "scandal" — like Peter we are inclined to "remonstrate" with our Savior over the mysterious way of salvation;
— Jesus falls but rises to move on to Calvary where he will fall in death
— but he will also rise from the dead.

For Myself

—to see my own moral falls as temporary moments to be overcome; to be warmhearted to others in their weakness and failure; to be fully and really compassionate.

FOURTH STATION

Is it nothing to you, all you who pass by? Look and see if there is any sorrow like my sorrow, which was brought upon me, which the LORD inflicted on the day of his fierce anger.
(Lamentations 1:12)

V. We adore you, O Christ, and we praise you.

R. Because by your holy cross you have redeemed the world.

Reflections

— Mary stood by Jesus in the last hours of his life as in his first hours;
— she was weeping but willing; she accepted his Father's will; she would gladly have suffered everything herself for us;
— for our sake she offers to the Father her Son, her maternal love, and her mother's rights.

For Myself

— to know and appreciate Mary's part in our redemption; to esteem her for her magnificent faith and her faithful love, not only for Jesus but for us whom she did not see or know.

FIFTH STATION

Simon Helps Jesus

Now as they were going out they found a man named Simon
of Cyrene; they forced this man to carry his cross.

(Matthew 27:32)

V. We adore you, O Christ, and we praise you.

R. Because by your holy cross you have redeemed the
world.

Reflections

— Simon is "enlisted" almost by chance or accident;
— the only memorable thing about Simon is that he
  helped a stranger to carry his cross to the place of
  execution;
— there is no indication that Jesus attempted to decline or
  refuse the help of Simon.

For Myself

— to make the works of mercy an important reality in my
  life; to see the image of Jesus in the suffering and the
  oppressed; to find my greatest fulfillment in selflessly
  helping others.

SIXTH STATION

VERONICA WIPES THE FACE OF JESUS

I gave my back to those who
    struck me,
and my cheeks to those who
    pulled out the beard;
I did not hide my face
    from insult and spitting.

(Isaiah 50:6)

V. We adore you, O Christ, and we praise you.
R. Because by your holy cross you have redeemed the
world.

Reflections

— the sufferings endured by Jesus are so terrible, the
    kindnesses shown him so few and so simple;
— Veronica, so far as we know, was not rich or popular or
    powerful -- but she was kind;
— how much this simple act must have been appreciated
    by Jesus.

For Myself

— to be zealous in doing the small kind service, in helping
    and healing in a modest way; to know the value of the
    seemingly minor comfort given to a brother or sister in
    need.

SEVENTH STATION

JESUS FALLS THE SECOND TIME

He himself bore our sins in his body on the cross, so that free from sins, we might live for righteousness; by his wounds you have been healed. For you were going astray like sheep, but now you have returned to the shepherd and guardian of your souls.

(1 Peter 2:24-25)

V. We adore you, O Christ, and we praise you.

R. Because by your holy cross you have redeemed the world.

Reflections

— the discouragement of repeated falls;
   — the abandonment Jesus must have felt;
   — he was carrying the burdens of us all.

For Myself

— to fight the repeated discouragements of "every day"; to know that we are never really abandoned by our Father in heaven; to have the strength to carry one another's burdens.

EIGHTH STATION

Jesus Speaks to the Women of Jerusalem

Now a large crowd of the people was following him, as well as women who were lamenting and wailing for him. But Jesus turned to them and said, **"Daughters of Jerusalem, don't weep for me; weep, instead, for yourselves and for your children, because, behold, the days are coming in which they'll say,**

> **'Blessed are those who are barren,**
> **and the wombs that did not give birth,**
> **and the breasts that did not nurse!'"**

(Luke 23:27-29)

V. We adore you, O Christ, and we praise you.
R. Because by your holy cross you have redeemed the world.

Reflections

— of themselves, mourning and lamentation accomplish little or nothing;
— to weep not for Jesus but for ourselves could lead to saving action;
— to weep for our children could lead to a lifestyle that would attract and intrigue them.

For Myself

— to resist the tendency to deplore and disdain the world because of its lack of faith; to move always toward positive goals for myself and others.

NINTH STATION

JESUS FALLS THE THIRD TIME

Surely he has borne our
    infirmities
  and carried our diseases;
yet we accounted him stricken,
  struck down by God, and
    afflicted.
But he was wounded for our
    transgressions,
  crushed for our iniquities;
upon him was the punishment
    that made us whole,
  and by his bruises we are
    healed.   (Isaiah 53:4-5)

V. We adore you, O Christ, and we praise you.
R. Because by your holy cross you have redeemed the
world.

Reflections

— how low Jesus is brought through repeated falls;
— how can this be the God-Man, the one who taught with
    authority, who defied the powerful and championed the
    weak?
— how can this be the one who will overcome death
    forever?

For Myself

— to retain my faith in Jesus, in my neighbor, and in
    myself, despite all the pitfalls of living; to be confident
    that even my weak flesh will not taste death forever.

TENTH STATION

Then they crucified him,
and his **clothes were divided up,
casting lots for them** to see
who would take what.

(Mark 15:24)

V. We adore you, O Christ, and we praise you.
R. Because by your holy cross you have redeemed the world.

Reflections

— Jesus is to be deprived of every last possession, to stand before his Father with literally nothing given him by this world;
— he will leave this world with nothing more than the flesh provided him by his mother;
— the most valuable act performed on this earth owes nothing to the world's goods.

For Myself

— to evaluate and constantly re-evaluate the things of earth in the light of faith; to use things without attachment; to be separated from things without grief for the sake of Christ.

ELEVENTH STATION

JESUS IS NAILED TO THE CROSS

Now after crucifying him "they divided his clothes among them by casting lots," and they sat down and kept watch over him there. And they placed the accusation against him over his head, which was written, "This is Jesus the King of the Jews." *(Matthew 27:35-37)*

V. We adore you, O Christ, and we praise you.
R. Because by your holy cross you have redeemed the world.

Reflections

— "Father, forgive them, for they do not know what they are doing."
— "This is Jesus, King of the Jews." How little they really knew!
— they kept guard over him, and all the time he was guarding them and us from eternal death.

For Myself

— to be forgiving even toward the truly guilty; to find my greatest honor in my freely willed union with Jesus; to refuse to be diverted by any purely human judgments.

TWELFTH STATION

JESUS DIES ON THE CROSS

And it was already about the sixth hour and darkness came over the whole land until the ninth hour, the sun having failed, while the sanctuary curtain was torn down the middle. And Jesus called out with a loud voice and said, **"Father, into your hands I entrust my spirit!"** And after saying this, he died.

V. We adore you, O Christ, and we praise you.
R. Because by your holy cross you have redeemed the world.

Reflections

— "It is finished" — the mysterious masterpiece is complete. Nothing has been omitted, nothing left undone.
— the model of trust at the time of death: "Father, into your hands I commend my spirit."
— he breathed his last in agony and he begins to pass to glory.

For Myself

— to overcome my natural repugnance to the thought of death; to so live that I may die with nothing consciously left undone; to entrust my spirit habitually to my Father's hands.

THIRTEENTH STATION

JESUS IS TAKEN DOWN FROM THE CROSS

Now when evening had come a rich man from Arimathea named Joseph, who had also been a disciple of Jesus, came; he went to Pilate and requested the body of Jesus. Then Pilate ordered it to be given to him.

(Matthew 27:57-58)

V. We adore you, O Christ, and we praise you.
R. Because by your holy cross you have redeemed the world.

Reflections

— Joseph of Arimathea provides an example of reverence;
— the care for the dead body of Jesus stands in sharp contrast with the needs that went unprovided before his death;
— Joseph, like Simon of Cyrene and Veronica, is known only for this single act of reverence.

For Myself

— to be merciful and compassionate in action; to care for the body of Christ, which is the Church, and for all the members of the body; to wish to be "known" above all for devotion to this body.

FOURTEENTH STATION

Jesus Is Laid in the Tomb

Joseph took the body and wrapped it in a clean linen shroud and placed it in his new tomb, which he had hewn in the rock, and after rolling a large stone up to the door of the tomb he went away. Now Mary Magdalen and the other Mary were there, sitting across from the sepulchre.

(Matthew 27:59-61)

V. We adore you, O Christ, and we praise you.
R. Because by your holy cross you have redeemed the world.

Reflections

— Joseph provides his own new tomb as a token and symbol of his discipleship;
— the value of anything we give for Jesus is in the dedicated heart that leads to the gift;
— the women watched, giving their time and themselves in their desire to remain with him.

For Myself

— to give to Jesus and for Jesus my constant allegiance and unity in will; to know that deeds and things take their real value from what is in my heart.

FIFTEENTH STATION

THE RESURRECTION

They were astonished. But he said to them, "Don't be alarmed; you're looking for Jesus the Nazarene who was crucified; he's risen, he's not here; look at the place where they placed him!" *(Mark 16:6)*

V. We adore you, O Christ, and we praise you.
R. Because by your holy cross you have redeemed the world.

Reflections

— Where is Jesus now? At his Father's right hand, present to all of us in his word, present among us at his eucharistic table and in the tabernacle, present wherever two or three are gathered in his name, present in his body which is the Church, in everyone who shares his Spirit.

For Myself

— to fill my day and my life with vitalizing contacts with the risen Jesus in his word, in the Eucharist and in my neighbor, as I move to join him at his Father's right hand.

PRIVATE HOLY HOUR

An hour of prayer and reflection before the blessed sacrament has proved for many people a most rewarding and revitalizing spiritual experience.

It is not necessary or even desirable to "construct" or outline precisely this hour of personal prayer. A person should, above all else, be open to the direction of the Holy Spirit, and in mind and heart follow the Spirit wherever it leads. If at first there is need for some help in order to focus one's prayerful thoughts, the following suggestions may be useful:

Read a selection in one of the gospels until some personal thought emerges which you then pursue; return to the gospel reading and continue it when you feel the first line of thought has been exhausted.

Begin the reflections on the mysteries of the rosary or the stations of the cross, as outlined in this prayer book. Again, pause to pursue any personalized thought that comes to mind.

Begin the private holy hour with the prayers given in the prayer book for before or after Mass.

Consider your holy hour as a leisurely preparation for, or thanksgiving after, Mass.

Reflect upon your own life — especially its sacramental moments — as a springboard toward spontaneous prayers of gratitude and petition to the heavenly Father.

AN ECUMENICAL SERVICE
THE WEEK OF PRAYER FOR CHRISTIAN UNITY

The following outline can be readily adapted
for a parish or regional service during the Week of Prayer
for Christian Unity.

THE ORDER OF SERVICE

Processional Hymn

Welcome

Call to Worship

V. O Lord, open my lips.
R. And my mouth shall proclaim your praise.

V. O God, come to my assistance.
R. O Lord, make haste to help me.

V. Glory be to the Father, and to the Son, and to the Holy Spirit.
R. As it was in the beginning, is now, and ever shall be, world without end. Amen.

Hymn

Prayer

Eternal God, who has called us to be members of one body: bind us to those who in all times and places have called upon

your name that, with one heart and mind, we may display the
unity of your Church, and bring glory to your Son, our
Savior, Jesus Christ. Amen.

(Book of Common Worship
of The United Presbyterian Church in the U.S.A.*)*

First Lesson

In days to come
> the mountain of the LORD'S house
> shall be established as the
>> highest of the mountains,
> and shall be raised up above the hills.

Peoples shall stream to it,
> and many nations shall come and say:
> "Come, let us go up to the
>> mountain of the LORD,
>> to the house of the God of Jacob;
> that he may teach us his ways
>> and that we may walk in his paths."

For out of Zion shall go forth instruction,
> and the word of the LORD from Jerusalem.

He shall judge between many peoples
> and shall arbitrate between strong nations far away;

they shall beat their swords into plowshares,
> and their spears into pruning hooks
> nation shall not lift up sword against nation,
>> neither shall they learn war any more;
> but they shall all sit under their own vines
>> and under their own fig trees,
> and not one shall make them afraid;
>> for the mouth of the LORD of hosts has spoken.

(Micah 4:1-4)

Time of Reflection

MEDITATION RESPONSE

All: Behold, how good it is, and how pleasant,
where brethren dwell as one!   *(Psalm 133:1)*

SECOND LESSON

Then Peter began to speak to them: "I truly understand that God shows no partiality, but in every nation anyone who fears him and does what is right is acceptable to him. You know the message he sent to the people of Israel, preaching peace by Jesus Christ — he is Lord of all. That message spread throughout Judea, beginning in Galilee after the baptism that John announced: how God anointed Jesus of Nazareth with the Holy Spirit and with power; how he went about doing good and healing all who were oppressed by the devil, for God was with him. We are witnesses to all that he did both in Judea and in Jerusalem. They put him to death by hanging him on a tree; but God raised him on the third day and allowed him to appear, not to all the people but to us who were chosen by God as witnesses, and who ate and drank with him after he rose from the dead. He commanded us to preach to the people and to testify that he is the one ordained by God as judge of the living and the dead. All the prophets testify about him that everyone who believes in him receives forgiveness of sins through his name."

While Peter was still speaking, the Holy Spirit fell upon all who heard the word. The circumcised believers who had come with Peter were astounded that the gift of the Holy Spirit had been poured out even on the Gentiles, for they heard them speaking in tongues and extolling God. Then

Peter said, "Can anyone withhold the water for baptizing these people who have received the Holy Spirit just as we have?" So he ordered them to be baptized in the name of Jesus Christ. Then they invited him to stay for several days.
(Acts 10:34-48)

"But when He comes — the Spirit of truth —
    He'll lead you to the whole truth,
For He won't speak on His own,
    but instead He'll say what He hears,
And He'll proclaim to you
    the things to come.
He'll glorify me because He'll receive what's mine
    and proclaim it to you.
Everything the Father has
    is mine;
That's why I said that He receives what's mine
    and proclaims it to you.

The Intercessor, the Holy Spirit the Father will send in my name, He'll teach you everything and will remind you of all the things I told you." *(John 16:13-15; 14:26)*

HYMN

SERMON

CONFESSION OF FAITH

Let the same mind be in you that was in Christ Jesus,
    who, though he was in the form of God
        did not regard equality with God
        as something to be exploited,

but emptied himself,
>   taking the form of a slave,
>   being born in human likeness.
And being found in human form,
>   he humbled himself
>   and became obedient to the point of death —
>   even death on a cross.
Therefore God also highly exalted him
>   and gave him the name
>   that is above every name,
so that at the name of Jesus
>   every knee should bend,
>   in heaven and on earth and under the earth,
and every tongue should confess
>   that JESUS CHRIST IS LORD,
>   to the glory of God the Father.

(Philippians 2:5-11)

INTERCESSIONS

Under the guidance of the Holy Spirit, may every Christian, every home, every church, every community, and every organization work for unity and love for all that God wills.
All: Lord, hear our prayer.

May we be strengthened in our confidence in the power of the Holy Spirit within the Church.
All: Lord, hear our prayer.

May the common good always be served by economic, social, religious, and political attitudes which acknowledge the dignity of the person and take into account the particular needs of this society.
All: Lord, hear our prayer.

May all people recognize God's plan in the universe and use wisely the discoveries of science for the benefit of individuals and nations.
All: Lord, hear our prayer.

May the Holy Spirit make us attentive to the cries of all who are not free because of political repression, racial discrimination, economic exploitation, or war.
All: Lord, hear our prayer.

May the Holy Spirit teach us to respect our heritage, and yet not to fear change where it is needed — in our churches, in our work, in our nation.
All: Lord, hear our prayer.

Trusting in the power of the Spirit to discern the truth, may we seek reconciliation with those who challenge our way of life, our loyalties, and our deepest beliefs.
All: Lord, hear our prayer.

Various Prayers

O God, the Father of our Lord Jesus Christ our only Savior, the Prince of Peace: give us grace seriously to lay to heart the great dangers we are in by our unhappy divisions. Take away all hatred and prejudice, and whatsoever else may hinder us from godly union and concord, that as there is but one Body and one Spirit, and one hope of our calling, one Lord, one faith, one baptism, one God and Father of us all, so we may be all of one heart and of one soul, united in one holy bond of truth and peace, of faith and charity, and may with one mind and one mouth glorify thee. Through Jesus Christ our Lord. Amen.   (*The Book of Common Prayer* of the Anglican Communion)

O God our Father, we truly desire the unity of your Church: help us to find your way to achieve it. Pour your Holy Spirit of love into our hearts, so that listening to each other without prejudice or mistrust, and knowing that we have nothing to fear from the truth, together we may find that Truth which is one. Help us to go forward day by day toward that perfect unity prayed for by Christ, your Son, when he said: "May they all be one. Father, may they be one in us, as you are in me, and I am in you, so that the world may believe it was you who sent me." Amen.   (*The Gustav Weigel Society*)

Almighty and eternal God, you keep together those you have united. Look kindly on all who follow Jesus your Son. We are all consecrated to you by our common baptism; make us one in the fullness of faith, and keep us one in the fellowship of love. Through Christ our Lord. Amen.

(The Roman Missal)

Let us sum up all our prayers in the words our Lord has taught us:

> Our Father, who art in heaven,
> > hallowed be thy name;
> > Thy kingdom come;
> > Thy will be done on earth as it is in heaven.
> Give us this day our daily bread;
> And forgive us our trespasses,
> > as we forgive those who trespass against us;
> And lead us not into temptation,
> > but deliver us from evil.
> For the kingdom, the power, and the glory are yours,
> > now and forever. Amen.

THE COMMITMENT
(*To be recited by the whole congregation*)

We accept our calling to make visible our unity in Christ. We commit ourselves to serve one another in love, not only in word, but in deed. In the coming year we shall strengthen our efforts to common action, prayer, and worship. Come, Holy Spirit, help us in this task.

THE BENEDICTION

The God of peace make us perfect in every good work to do his will, working in us that which is well-pleasing in his sight. Through Jesus Christ, to whom be the glory for ever and ever. Amen.

RECESSIONAL HYMN

ALTERNATE GOSPEL READING

"But to you who are listening, I say,

> Love your enemies,
> > do good to those who hate you,
> Bless those who curse you,
> > pray for those who insult you.
> To the one who strikes you on one cheek,
> > offer the other cheek as well,
> And from the one who takes your cloak,
> > don't hold back your tunic.
> Give to all who ask of you,
> > and don't demand what's yours
> > from him who took it.
> And as you wish others to do for you,
> > do likewise for them.

If you love those who love you,
    what kindness is that in you?
For sinners also love those who love them.

And if you do good to those who do good to you,
    what kindness is that in you?
Sinners also do the same.

And if you lend to those from whom you
    expect to receive,
    what kindness is there in you?
Sinners also lend to sinners, to get back
    equal amounts.

But love those who hate you,
    and do good and lend expecting nothing,
And your reward will be great,
    and you'll be sons of the Most High,
Because He's kind to the ungrateful
    and the evil.

Be merciful,
    as your Father is merciful.
And don't judge,
    and you won't be judged;
And don't condemn,
    and you won't be condemned.
Forgive,
    and you will be forgiven,
Give,
    and it will be given to you.
Good measure,
    pressed down, shaken together,
Overflowing,
    they shall give into your bosom,

For with the measure you measure
  it will be measured out to you in return."

He also told them a parable.

"Can a blind man lead a blind man?
Won't they both fall into a ditch?

A disciple is not above his teacher but, when fully trained, each disciple will be like his teacher.

But why do you see the speck in your brother's eye,
    yet don't notice the log in your own eye?
Or how can you say to your brother, 'Brother, let me
    take out the speck in your eye!'
    while you don't see the log in your own eye?
Hypocrite!
First take the log out of your own eye,
    and *then* you'll see clearly to take out the speck
    in your brother's eye."   *(Luke 6:27-42)*

SACRED LITANIES

LITANY OF THE SACRED HEART OF JESUS

Lord, have mercy on us.
Christ, have mercy on us.

Lord, have mercy on us.
Christ, graciously hear us.

God the Father of heaven, *have mercy on us.*
God the Son, Redeemer of the world, *have mercy on us.*
God the Holy Spirit, *have mercy on us.*
Holy Trinity, one God, *have mercy on us.*

Heart of Jesus, Son of the Eternal Father, *have mercy on us.*
Heart of Jesus, formed by the Holy Spirit in the womb of the
Virgin Mother, *have mercy on us.*
Heart of Jesus, united substantially with the Word of God,
  have mercy on us.
Heart of Jesus, of infinite majesty, *have mercy on us.*
Heart of Jesus, holy temple of God, *have mercy on us.*
Heart of Jesus, tabernacle of the Most High, *have mercy on us.*
Heart of Jesus, house of God and gate of heaven,
  have mercy on us.
Heart of Jesus, glowing furnace of charity, *have mercy on us.*
Heart of Jesus, vessel of justice and love, *have mercy on us.*
Heart of Jesus, full of goodness and love, *have mercy on us.*
Heart of Jesus, abyss of all virtues, *have mercy on us.*
Heart of Jesus, most worthy of all praise, *have mercy on us.*
Heart of Jesus, king and center of all hearts, *have mercy on us.*
Heart of Jesus, in whom are all the treasures of wisdom and
  knowledge, *have mercy on us.*
Heart of Jesus, in whom dwells all the fullness of divinity,
  have mercy on us.

Heart of Jesus, in whom the Father is well pleased,
>   *have mercy on us.*

Heart of Jesus, of whose fullness we have all received, *have mercy on us.*

Heart of Jesus, desire of the eternal hills, *have mercy on us.*

Heart of Jesus, patient and rich in mercy, *have mercy on us.*

Heart of Jesus, rich to all who invoke you, *have mercy on us.*

Heart of Jesus, fount of life and holiness, *have mercy on us.*

Heart of Jesus, propitiation for our sins, *have mercy on us.*

Heart of Jesus, loaded down with opprobrium,
>   *have mercy on us.*

Heart of Jesus, bruised for our offenses, *have mercy on us.*

Heart of Jesus, made obedient unto death, *have mercy on us.*

Heart of Jesus, pierced with a lance, *have mercy on us.*

Heart of Jesus, source of all consolation, *have mercy on us.*

Heart of Jesus, our life and resurrection, *have mercy on us.*

Heart of Jesus, our peace and reconciliation, *have mercy on us.*

Heart of Jesus, victim for our sin, *have mercy on us.*

Heart of Jesus, salvation of those who hope in you,
>   *have mercy on us.*

Heart of Jesus, hope of those who die in you,
>   *have mercy on us.*

Heart of Jesus, delight of all the saints, *have mercy on us.*

Lamb of God, who takes away the sins of the world,
>   *spare us, O Lord.*

Lamb of God, who takes away the sins of the world,
>   *graciously hear us, O Lord.*

Lamb of God, who takes away the sins of the world,
>   *have mercy on us.*

V. Jesus, meek and humble of heart.

R. Make our hearts like unto yours.

LET US PRAY

Almighty and everlasting God, graciously regard the heart of your well-beloved Son and the acts of praise and satisfaction which he renders you on behalf of us sinners; and through their merit, grant pardon to us who implore your mercy, in the name of your Son, Jesus Christ, who lives and reigns with you in the unity of the Holy Spirit, one God, world without end. Amen.

LITANY OF THE BLESSED VIRGIN

Lord, have mercy on us.
Christ, have mercy on us.

Lord, have mercy on us. Christ hear us.
Christ, graciously hear us.

God the Father of heaven, *have mercy on us.*
God the Son, Redeemer of the world, *have mercy on us.*
God the Holy Spirit, *have mercy on us.*
Holy Trinity, one God, *have mercy on us.*
Holy Mary, *pray for us.*
Holy Mother of God, *pray for us.*
Holy Virgin of virgins, *pray for us.*
Mother of Christ, *pray for us.*
Mother of the Church, *pray for us.*
Mother of divine grace, *pray for us.*
Mother most pure, *pray for us.*
Mother most chaste, *pray for us.*
Mother inviolate, *pray for us.*
Mother undefiled, *pray for us.*
Mother most amiable, *pray for us.*
Mother most admirable, *pray for us.*
Mother of good counsel, *pray for us.*

Mother of our Creator, *pray for us.*
Mother of our Savior, *pray for us.*
Virgin most prudent, *pray for us.*
Virgin most venerable, *pray for us.*
Virgin most renowned, *pray for us.*
Virgin most powerful, *pray for us.*
Virgin most merciful, *pray for us.*
Virgin most faithful, *pray for us.*
Mirror of justice, *pray for us.*
Seat of wisdom, *pray for us.*
Cause of our joy, *pray for us.*
Spiritual vessel, *pray for us.*
Vessel of honor, *pray for us.*
Vessel of singular devotion, *pray for us.*
Mystical rose, *pray for us.*
Tower of David, *pray for us.*
Tower of ivory, *pray for us.*
House of gold, *pray for us.*
Ark of the covenant, *pray for us.*
Gate of heaven, *pray for us.*
Morning star, *pray for us.*
Health of the sick, *pray for us.*
Refuge of sinners, *pray for us.*
Comforter of the afflicted, *pray for us.*
Help of Christians, *pray for us.*
Queen of Angels, *pray for us.*
Queen of Patriarchs, *pray for us.*
Queen of Prophets, *pray for us.*
Queen of Apostles, *pray for us.*
Queen of Martyrs, *pray for us.*
Queen of Confessors, *pray for us.*
Queen of Virgins, *pray for us.*
Queen of all Saints, *pray for us.*

Queen conceived without original sin, *pray for us.*
Queen assumed into heaven, *pray for us.*
Queen of the most holy rosary, *pray for us.*
Queen of peace, *pray for us.*

Lamb of God, who takes away the sins of the world,
    spare us, O Lord.
Lamb of God, who takes away the sins of the world,
    graciously hear us, O Lord.
Lamb of God, who takes away the sins of the world,
    have mercy on us.

V. Pray for us, O holy Mother of God.
R. That we may be made worthy of the promises of Christ.

LET US PRAY

Grant, we beseech you, O Lord God, that we, your servants, may enjoy perpetual health of soul and body; and by the glorious intercession of blessed Mary, ever virgin, may be delivered from present sorrows and rejoice in eternal happiness. Through Christ, our Lord. Amen.

LITANY OF THE MOST HOLY NAME OF JESUS

Lord, have mercy.
Christ, have mercy.

Lord, have mercy. Jesus hear us.
Jesus, graciously hear us.

God the Father of heaven, *have mercy on us.*
God the Son, Redeemer of the world, *have mercy on us.*
God the Holy Spirit, *have mercy on us.*
Holy Trinity, one God, *have mercy on us.*

Jesus, Son of the living God, *have mercy on us.*
Jesus, splendor of the Father, *have mercy on us.*
Jesus, brightness of eternal light, *have mercy on us.*
Jesus, King of Glory, *have mercy on us.*
Jesus, Sun of Justice, *have mercy on us.*
Jesus, Son of the Virgin Mary, *have mercy on us.*
Jesus, most amiable, *have mercy on us.*
Jesus, most admirable, *have mercy on us.*
Jesus, mighty God, *have mercy on us.*
Jesus, Father of the world to come, *have mercy on us.*
Jesus, Angel of great counsel, *have mercy on us.*
Jesus, most powerful, *have mercy on us.*
Jesus, most patient, *have mercy on us.*
Jesus, most obedient, *have mercy on us.*
Jesus, meek and humble of heart, *have mercy on us.*
Jesus, lover of chastity, *have mercy on us.*
Jesus, lover of us, *have mercy on us.*
Jesus, God of peace, *have mercy on us.*
Jesus, author of life, *have mercy on us.*
Jesus, example of all virtues, *have mercy on us.*
Jesus, zealous lover of souls, *have mercy on us.*
Jesus, our God, *have mercy on us.*
Jesus, our refuge, *have mercy on us.*
Jesus, Father of the poor, *have mercy on us.*
Jesus, treasure of the faithful, *have mercy on us.*
Jesus, Good Shepherd, *have mercy on us.*
Jesus, true light, *have mercy on us.*
Jesus, eternal wisdom, *have mercy on us.*
Jesus, infinite goodness, *have mercy on us.*
Jesus, our way, our truth and our life, *have mercy on us.*
Jesus, joy of the angels, *have mercy on us.*
Jesus, King of Patriarchs, *have mercy on us.*
Jesus, master of the apostles, *have mercy on us.*

Jesus, teacher of the evangelists, *have mercy on us.*
Jesus, strength of martyrs, *have mercy on us.*
Jesus, light of confessors, *have mercy on us.*
Jesus, purity of virgins, *have mercy on us.*
Jesus, crown of all saints, *have mercy on us.*

Be merciful to us: *Spare us, O Jesus.*
Be merciful to us: *Graciously hear us, O Jesus.*

From all evil, *O Jesus, deliver us.*
From all sin, *O Jesus, deliver us.*
From your wrath, *O Jesus, deliver us.*
From the snares of the devil, *O Jesus, deliver us.*
From the spirit of fornication, *O Jesus, deliver us.*
From everlasting death, *O Jesus, deliver us.*
From the neglect of your inspiration, *O Jesus, deliver us.*
Through the mystery of your holy Incarnation,
    O Jesus, deliver us.
Through your nativity, *O Jesus, deliver us.*
Through your infancy, *O Jesus, deliver us.*
Through your most divine life, *O Jesus, deliver us.*
Through your labors, *O Jesus, deliver us.*
Through your agony and passion, *O Jesus, deliver us.*
Through your cross and dereliction, *O Jesus, deliver us.*
Through your pains and torments, *O Jesus, deliver us.*
Through your death and burial, *O Jesus, deliver us.*
Through your Resurrection, *O Jesus, deliver us.*
Through your Ascension, *O Jesus, deliver us.*
Through your institution of the most Holy Eucharist,
    O Jesus, deliver us.
Through your glory, *O Jesus, deliver us.*

Lamb of God, who takes away the sins of the world,
    spare us, O Jesus.

Lamb of God, who takes away the sins of the world, *graciously hear us, O Jesus.*
Lamb of God, who takes away the sins of the world, *have mercy on us, O Jesus.*

Jesus, hear us.
Jesus, graciously hear us.

Let Us Pray

O Lord, Jesus Christ, who said: "Ask and you shall receive; seek and you shall find; knock and it shall be opened unto you," give, we beseech you, to us who ask, the grace of your most divine love, that with all our hearts, words, and works, we may love you and never cease to praise you. Make us, O Lord, to have an abiding fear and love of your holy name, for never does your providence abandon those whom you firmly establish in your love. Who lives and reigns world without end. Amen.

LITANY OF THE SAINTS

Lord, have mercy on us.
Lord, have mercy on us.

Christ, have mercy on us.
Christ, have mercy on us.

Lord, have mercy on us.
Lord, have mercy on us.

Holy Mary, Mother of God, *pray for us.*
St. Michael, *pray for us.*
Holy angels of God, *pray for us.*
St. Joseph, *pray for us.*

St. John the Baptist, *pray for us.*

St. Peter and St. Paul, *pray for us.*

St. Andrew, *pray for us.*

St. John, *pray for us.*

St. Mary Magdalene, *pray for us.*

St. Stephen, *pray for us.*

St. Ignatius, *pray for us.*

St. Lawrence, *pray for us.*

St. Perpetua and St. Felicity, *pray for us.*

St. Agnes, *pray for us.*

St. Gregory, *pray for us.*

St. Augustine, *pray for us.*

St. Athanasius, *pray for us.*

St. Basil, *pray for us.*

St. Martin, *pray for us.*

St. Benedict, *pray for us.*

St. Francis and St. Dominic, *pray for us.*

St. Francis Xavier, *pray for us.*

St. John Vianney, *pray for us.*

St. Catherine, *pray for us.*

St. Theresa, *pray for us.*

All you saints of God, *pray for us.*

Lord, be merciful. *Lord, save us.*

From all harm, *Lord, save us.*

From every sin, *Lord, save us.*

From all temptations, *Lord, save us.*

From everlasting death, *Lord, save us.*

By your coming among us, *Lord, save us.*

By your death and rising to new life, *Lord, save us.*

By your gift of the Holy Spirit, *Lord, save us.*

Be merciful to us sinners. *Lord, hear our prayer.*

Guide and protect your holy Church, *Lord, hear our prayer.*

Keep our pope and all the clergy in faithful service to your

Church, *Lord, hear our prayer.*
Bring all peoples together in trust and peace, *Lord, hear our prayer.*
Strengthen us in your service, *Lord, hear our prayer.*

Let Us Pray

From you, Lord, comes holiness in our desires, right thinking in our plans, and justice in our actions. Grant your children that peace which the world cannot give; then our hearts will be devoted to your laws, we shall be delivered from the terrors of war and, under your protection, we shall be able to live in tranquillity. Through Christ our Lord. Amen.

A COMMUNAL PENANCE SERVICE

Penance Becomes You

My God, accept my heart this day
And keep it wholly true,
That I by sin no more may stray,
No more depart from you.

Before the cross of him who died,
Behold I humbly fall;
Let every wrong be crucified,
Let Christ be all in all.

In some degree, I have known how lonely it can be, once I have alienated myself from God through sin. In fact, I have also known how lonely it can be to be alienated from those with whom I enjoyed a common faith and love of God, because sin had alienated me from them as well. Jesus has been a Redeemer to me, again and again, from my baptism through every reconciliation I have known. At this moment, I stand in his presence, and once again claim his mercy. Both deserving of punishment and confident of forgiveness, I call upon the Lord who is merciful.

O God, intensify within us a sense of responsibility to you and to one another. The cross and the empty tomb are the signs of your unfailing forgiveness. The sacrament of penance is the sign of your forgiving activity among us. In asking your forgiveness, and in being confident that you will grant it, may we be signs to a world that needs forgiveness. Through Christ our Lord. Amen.

SUGGESTED READINGS

Ezekiel 36:25-31 (except vv. 29 and 30), "I shall give you a new heart."
Isaiah 40:1-5, "Prepare a way for our God."
Isaiah 1:15-18, "Wash and purify yourselves."
Matthew 5:1-10, "The Beatitudes."
Matthew 7:21-27, "Put into practice the will of God."
John 10:7-18, "The Good Shepherd."

Recite: *The Lord's Prayer* and *The Act of Contrition.*

Individual Confession and Absolution

THANKSGIVING

Father, it is our duty and our salvation always and everywhere to give you thanks through your beloved Son, Jesus Christ. You seek not the death of sinners, but rather their conversion, so that they may be more fully alive. Be merciful to your people and, as you give us the grace to serve you, make us new with your loving help, through Jesus Christ, your Son, our Lord, who lives and reigns with you in the unity of the Holy Spirit, one God, for ever and ever. Amen.

Prayer for Examination

You have called us to conversion and contrition
— but we have been so indifferent;
— but we have made so small an effort to change our hearts, and to adjust our way of living.
You have shown us how to share with those in need
— but we have so often refused to share our time or resources, or even our joy and our friendship, with others;
— but we have so often allowed others to go hungry.
Through your Son, you became one of us and lived in our midst
— but we have worked so little in remaking a world which would reflect your justice and your peace;
— but we have said so little about your Good News.
You sat in the home of the tax collector and were the open friend of sinners
— but we have been so concerned about status, about the way things look;
— but we have hesitated to establish real relations with our neighbor.
You have shown us how to love
— but we do not love, or do not love enough;
— we do not come up to expectations, even our own;
— we contribute to hatred, and hardness, and dishonesty;
— and reveal a lack of trust and understanding;

— we are quick to criticize, even though we contribute to the misunderstanding;
— we live through days of indifference and tension,
— and contribute to a climate of suspicion;
— we overemphasize the unimportant,
— and act upon our first impressions;
— we insist on *our* rights, come what may,
— embarrass others when we should be embarrassed,
— and portray a picture of intolerance.

Also see *Points of Reference for the Examination of Conscience,* page 116.

PART 3

PRAYERS REVEALING
THE HEART OF CARDINAL COOKE

FIAT VOLUNTAS TUA

These prayers were composed by Cardinal Cooke after the publication of the first edition of this prayer book. Though they were penned for special occasions, they reflect the broad range of interest in the day-to-day lives of the persons and groups for whom they were written. As such they tell us much about the loving and gentle character of the man who wrote them.

A PRAYER FOR FAMILIES

Lord, Heavenly Father, hear our prayer for family life.

Enlighten our minds to see clearly that we are
    all brothers and sisters in You.

Make us more sensitive to each other's pains and needs
    and more aware that wherever suffering exists
    — at home or in far-off countries —
    we cannot be indifferent.

Increase our faith and enable us
    to touch each other's lives
    with understanding and with hope.

Help us to be true members of Your family,
    saved by Your infinite love
    and determined to share that love
    by being instruments of joy and peace to the world.

Give us the courage to accomplish Your Will
    as we celebrate the birth of Your Son, Jesus Christ.
      Amen.

PRAYER FOR MEMBERS OF THE PRESS

O Lord,
we ask you to bless
the members of the press
in their many hopes and endeavors.

Bless us,
O Heavenly Father,
in our resolve to *tell the truth*
which *You alone possess in fulness.*

May we distill
from the flood of world events,
the heart of reality
and a wisdom that will be *a light to our people*.
Keep before our minds
the *importance* of the knowledge we give
to those who by their decisions
can lead whole nations to happiness and peace.

Lord,
You have placed the safety of your people
in the hands of those who *report the truth*.
Direct the steps of men and women
who every day
seek that truth,
edit its release,
and publish it in ways that
serve and *guide* our world.

Grant us,
Heavenly Father,
the promise of the Prophet who said:

"... You shall delight in the Almighty
and you shall lift up your face toward God
... and upon *your ways* the *light* shall shine."

(Job 22:26-27)

Keep us heirs and custodians
of the light of truth
which frees all people from fear
and leads them to the service of their neighbor.

Bless all those who gather in friendship
and solidarity. Amen.

PRAYER FOR PHYSICIANS

Eternal Father, we pray for the men and women to whom the wondrous skill has been given to heal the human body and, by so doing, to also touch the human heart; let them always be conscious of You and of Your own provident care for all the members of Your human family.

Eternal Father, give them a deep and abiding respect for life from the moment of its conception to the moment when You decree its passing into eternity. Give them a love of life, a gentleness in caring for the young and the old, the sick and the dying, the fearful and the brave.

Eternal Father, as this world becomes ever more complicated and medicine becomes ever more scientific; as treatment becomes more extensive — and more intensive — involving surgeons of the body and doctors of the mind, generalists and specialists and social workers too, renew in each of us the basic commitment to the dignity of the human person, the dedication to the individual patient, the willing generous love of the brother or sister whose life is in our hands. Amen.

PRAYER FOR FIRE AND POLICE PERSONNEL

Heavenly Father,
Protector of Your People,
bless we beseech You
all the men and women who have served
and still serve in the Fire and Police Departments.

In this time of increasing dangers and difficulties
instill within these officers and personnel

the special virtues of fortitude,
patience and dedicated service.

We thank You, Almighty God,
by whom all courage is sustained,
for the contributions which these men and women have
     made
to the communities which they serve
so fearlessly and so faithfully.
Their presence and ready response
assures the security and tranquility of peaceful
     communities,
and is an heroic contribution
to cities in turmoil.

Protect them, we pray,
against dangers which ever lie in wait
for those who think of their dedication before themselves.
Shield them from bodily harm.
Fill them with the high-mindedness they need
when they are neglected or abused.
Keep in their minds the wholesome example
that their sense of duty,
their reliability,
and their ready sacrifices
offer to the youth of our nation.

Bless them all, we beg You.
Bless their families,
their associates,
and bless forever
those who have given their lives
to protect our communities. Amen.

PRAYER FOR THE PRESIDENT

O Heavenly Father, we thank You on this historic day for all the blessings that You have bestowed upon our country from its very beginning up to the present moment. In Your fatherly care, You have endowed America not only with abundant physical resources but more especially with the spiritual resources of honorable and dedicated public servants who have pursued the noble goal of "liberty and justice for all."

We thank You, O Father in heaven, for the generous spirit in our society that makes possible a peaceful and orderly change of administration. Aware as we are of the challenges that face us and the problems that could divide us, we pray that under Your guidance we may remain a people united, a nation indivisible. We pray that You will ever foster in each of us the breadth of vision, the depth of conviction, and the oneness of purpose which have been the greatest glories of our nation's history. May we now use this blessed heritage to assure peace, equality, and dignity for every person in our beloved land.

We are aware, O Heavenly Father, that our nation bears a special responsibility of leadership among nations for the future peace of all on earth. Enlighten us to discover Your will for our world today, and strengthen us to be courageous in fulfilling it. May we find our true destiny and our lasting happiness in the loving service of our brothers and sisters everywhere — in being neighbors to each and every one we meet.

O Merciful Father, bless the devoted leaders who have led our nation in the years past and those who will guide it in the years to come. Help them, we humbly pray, to bear the great burdens of their office; be to them a consolation and inspiration. And may each of us daily raise our minds and hearts to You, imploring Your blessing upon our President, his Vice President, his family, and all who will assist him in the work of his great office.

Father of our human race, may our President have the wholehearted support of all his fellow Americans in his efforts to serve You, our country and our world. Amen.

A CHRISTMAS PRAYER FOR CHILDREN

Heavenly Father, Christmas is Your special gift to children. They have the simple, all-important virtues of this day: the Christmas spirit of joy and good cheer, of giving and receiving. They radiate the peace, love and happiness of this family feast day.

Heavenly Father of Children, guard these Your little ones in the days to come. Inspire and strengthen us to protect their love and their hopes by our faithfulness to Your word. Make us willing to work and sacrifice so that they may live in the peace and dignity You intend for the members of Your family. And may all of us continue to grow in the awareness that You are indeed our Father and we are the members of Your one human family.

Heavenly Father, our hope and prayer at Christmas is that all of us in our beloved country and throughout the world will strive to live together in joy, love and peace as Your children and members of Your family during this Holy Season and throughout the New Year.

PRAYER DEDICATING ARCHDIOCESE TO MARY

Holy Mary, Mother of the Lord and Mother of the Church, accept our prayers to you as we celebrate the anniversary of this family of New York which Your Son has called into being.

To you, who are Mother of the Church, we dedicate on this special day the whole Church of New York. We thank you for your loving protection in the past one hundred seventy-five years.

For this Church in New York, we ask that you always show yourself as Mother: inspire all of us to obey your Son by acts of love and service to all our brothers and sisters.

Hear this our prayer of dedication to you, and open our eyes to the presence of Your Son in our midst: in His Holy Word and in the gift of His Sacraments.

Make us always sensitive to Jesus as He gives Himself to us in a special way through those in need, and Most Holy Mother, give us the inspiration to respond to His presence.

You are enthroned in the glory of your Son, sharing the victory of His Cross and Resurrection over the powers of this world. Watch over us, and guide us, as we make the journey of our earthly lives to that everlasting Kingdom where you reign as Queen. Holy Mary, Mother of God, pray for us sinners, now, and at the hour of death. Amen.

PART 4

FAMILIAR PRAYERS FOR READY REFERENCE

FIAT VOLUNTAS TUA

THE SIGN OF THE CROSS

In the name of the Father, and of the Son, and of the Holy Spirit. Amen.

THE LORD'S PRAYER

Our Father, who art in heaven, hallowed be thy name; thy kingdom come; thy will be done on earth as it is in heaven. Give us this day our daily bread; and forgive us our trespasses, as we forgive those who trespass against us; and lead us not into temptation, but deliver us from evil. Amen.

THE HAIL MARY

Hail Mary, full of grace; the Lord is with you; blessed are you among women, and blessed is the fruit of your womb, Jesus. Holy Mary, Mother of God, pray for us sinners, now and at the hour of our death. Amen.

THE GLORIA

Glory be to the Father, and to the Son, and to the Holy Spirit; as it was in the beginning, is now, and ever shall be, world without end. Amen.

THE APOSTLES' CREED

I believe in God, the Father almighty, Creator of heaven and earth; and in Jesus Christ, his only Son, our Lord: who was conceived by the Holy Spirit, born of the Virgin Mary, suffered under Pontius Pilate, was crucified, died, and was buried. He descended into hell; the third day he rose again from the dead. He ascended into heaven, and sits at the right hand of God, the Father almighty; from thence he shall come to judge the living and the dead. I believe in the Holy Spirit, the holy Catholic Church, the communion of saints, the forgiveness of sins, the resurrection of the body, and life everlasting. Amen.

HAIL, HOLY QUEEN (SALVE, REGINA)

Hail, holy Queen, Mother of mercy, our life, our sweetness, and our hope! To you do we cry, poor banished children of Eve! To you do we send up our sighs, mourning and weeping in this vale of tears. Turn then, most gracious advocate, your eyes of mercy toward us; and after this our exile, show us the blessed fruit of your womb, Jesus. O clement, O loving, O sweet Virgin Mary! Pray for us, O holy Mother of God, that we may be made worthy of the promises of Christ.

The preceding prayers are used in praying the rosary. The Our Father *is said on all single beads, the* Hail Mary *is said for each bead in the decade. The* Gloria *is used at the end of each decade. The* Sign of the Cross *and the* Apostles' Creed *are used to begin the rosary, and the* Hail, Holy Queen *is said at its conclusion.*

For reflections on the mysteries of the rosary, see pages 119-132.

THE CONFITEOR

I confess to almighty God, to blessed Mary, ever Virgin, to blessed Michael the Archangel, to blessed John the Baptist, to the holy apostles Peter and Paul, and to all the saints, that I have sinned exceedingly in thought, word, and deed;

through my fault, through my fault, through my most grievous fault. Therefore I beseech blessed Mary, ever Virgin, blessed Michael the Archangel, blessed John the Baptist, the holy apostles Peter and Paul, and all the saints, to pray to the Lord our God for me.

ACT OF CONTRITION

O my God, I am heartily sorry for having offended you. I detest all my sins, because I dread the loss of heaven and the pains of hell, but most of all because they offend you, my God, who are all-good, and deserving of all my love. I firmly resolve, with the help of your grace, to confess my sins, to do penance, and to amend my life. Amen.

ACT OF FAITH

O my God, I firmly believe that you are one God in three divine Persons: the Father, the Son, and the Holy Spirit; I believe that the divine Son became man, and died for our sins, and that he will come to judge the living and the dead. I believe these and all the truths which the holy Catholic Church teaches, because you have revealed them, who can neither deceive nor be deceived.

ACT OF HOPE

O my God, relying on your infinite goodness and promises, I hope to obtain pardon of my sins, the help of your grace and life everlasting, through the merits of Jesus Christ, my Lord and Redeemer.

ACT OF CHARITY

O my God, I love you above all things, with my whole heart and soul, because you are all good and worthy of all love. I love my neighbor as myself for love of you. I forgive all who have injured me and ask pardon of all whom I have injured.

DIVINE PRAISES

Blessed be God.
Blessed be his holy name.
Blessed be Jesus Christ, true God and true man.
Blessed be the name of Jesus.
Blessed be his most sacred heart.
Blessed be his most precious blood.
Blessed be Jesus in the most holy sacrament of the altar.
Blessed be the Holy Spirit, the Paraclete.
Blessed be the great Mother of God, Mary most holy.
Blessed be her holy and Immaculate Conception.
Blessed be her glorious Assumption.
Blessed be the name of Mary, virgin and mother.
Blessed be St. Joseph, her most chaste spouse.
Blessed be God in his angels and in his saints.

THREE MORNING OFFERINGS

At the beginning of each day, I speak in my mind and heart with my heavenly Father and offer to him the whole of the day he has given me.

I believe, O God, that I am in your presence, that you watch over me and listen to my prayers. You are so great and so holy, I adore you. You have given me all, I thank you. You have been so offended by me, I ask your pardon with all my heart. You are so merciful and I ask of you all the graces which you know will be beneficial to me.

O Jesus, through the Immaculate Heart of Mary, I offer you my prayers, works, joys and sufferings of this day in union with the holy sacrifice of the Mass throughout the world. I offer them for all the intentions of your Sacred Heart: the salvation of souls, reparation for sin, the union of all Christians. I offer them for the intentions of our bishops and of all apostles of prayer, and in particular for those recommended by our Holy Father this month.

Eternal Father, I offer you everything I do this day: my work, my prayers, my apostolic efforts; my time with family and friends; my hours of relaxation; my difficulties, problems, distresses, which I shall try to bear with patience. Join these, my gifts, to the unique offering which Jesus Christ, your Son, renews today in the Eucharist.

GRACE BEFORE MEALS

Bless us, O Lord, and these your gifts, which we are about to receive from your bounty, through Christ our Lord. Amen.

THE ANGELUS

V. The Angel of the Lord declared unto Mary.
R. And she conceived of the Holy Spirit.

Hail Mary, etc.

V. Behold the handmaid of the Lord.
R. Be it done unto me according to your word.

Hail Mary, etc.

V. And the Word was made flesh.
R. And dwelt among us.

Hail Mary, etc.

V. Pray for us, O holy Mother of God.
R. That we may be made worthy of the promises of Christ.

Let us pray: Pour forth, we beseech you, O Lord, your grace into our hearts that we, to whom the Incarnation of Christ, your Son, was made known by the message of an angel, may, by his passion and cross, be brought to the glory of his resurrection. Through the same Christ, our Lord. Amen.

THE MEMORARE

Remember, O most compassionate Virgin Mary, that never was it known that anyone who fled to your protection, implored your help, or sought your intercession, was left unaided. Inspired by this confidence I fly unto you, O Virgin of virgins, my Mother. To you do I come, before you I kneel, sinful and sorrowful. O Mother of the Word Incarnate, despise not my petitions in my necessities, but in your mercy, hear and answer them. Amen.